Minnesota's Lost Towns
CENTRAL EDITION

T0099260

Also by Rhonda Fochs

Minnesota's Lost Towns Northern Edition

Minnesota's Lost Towns Northern Edition II

Minnesota's Lost Towns Southern Edition

Wisconsin's Lost Towns

Minnesota's Lost Towns

CENTRAL EDITION

Rhonda Fochs

NORTH STAR PRESS OF ST. CLOUD, IN.
St. Cloud, Minnesota

Copyright © 2015 Rhonda Fochs

All rights reserved.

ISBN 978-0-87839-804-1

Printed in the United States of America.

Published by:
North Star Press of St. Cloud, Inc.
St. Cloud, Minnesota

www.northstarpress.com

ACKNOWLEDGMENTS

Without the assistance, help, and support of many, many people and organizations, this book would not have been possible. Early historians, known and unknown, writing local and family histories left for later generations, an invaluable record of the times and people of the past. Their written works, letters, oral and written histories are a treasure-trove of memories, tales, anecdotes, and facts that would be lost without their foresight and their efforts to record them. Without their contributions, we would be severely limited in our knowledge of and the rich details of the past. It is a great debt that I—that we—owe to those early historians.

I can't stress enough the importance of local historical societies and museums. These local repositories are true gems right in the midst of our local communities. With limited funds and resources, the staff and volunteers of these organizations preserve our past and ensure our future. I urge you to visit them, support them and perhaps even volunteer. Without them, and the people involved with them, we would be sorely lacking in our historical knowledge and legacy. Libraries are equally important. This book could not have been written without them.

To my family and friends, I thank you for your belief, support and your help in so many ways. Special thanks to Marlys Vollegraf, a true wordsmith and friend.

To those that allowed me the use of their photos, thank you. Your credits are listed by your photos.

Should I have inadvertently omitted anyone, my apologies. Any omission was purely unintentional. Again, thank you.

ORGANIZATIONS:
Anoka County Historical Society
Arcola Mills Historic Foundation
Benton County Historical Society
Big Stone County Historical Society
Carver County Historical Society
Chippewa County Historical Society
Constance Free Church
Franconia Sculpture Park
Franconia Town Board
Glen Cary Church
Great River Regional Library
Hassan Area Historical Society
Isanti County Historical Society
Kanabec History Center
Kandiyohi Historical Society
Laq Qui Parle Historical Society
Little Log House Pioneer Village
McLeod County Historical Society
Meeker County Historical Society
MNLINK
Padua Pub
Renville County Historical Society
Sherburne History Center
Sibley County Historical Society
Staples Library
Stearns History Center
Swift County Historical Society
Washington County Historical Society
Watab Township Board
WJON
Wright County Historical Society
Yellowmaps.com

INDIVIDUALS:
Dean E. Abrahamson
Marlyn and Sandra Johnson
Wally Anderson
Linda Balk
Betty Barrett
Terry Berglin
Travis Bonovsky
Vanessa Bowen
Marilyn Braun
Corinne Brevick
Wendy Brion
Evonne Brooton
Arlene Busse
Alton Chermak
Kathryn Draeger
Marlys Gallagher
Mo Galvin
Andrew Gaylord
Robert Gaylord
Mary and John Gilbertson
Melissa Glenna
Heidi Gould
Delores Hagen
Sharon Haggenmiller
Ashley Hanson
Jane Hanson
Carol Harker
Larry Helgeson
Adell Hofer
Sandy Johnson
Sue Jorgenson
Marjorie LaTour
Lisa Lenarz
Audrey LeVasseur
Karolyn Lindberg
Tim Lyon

Todd Mahon
Shelby Matula
Gerry Moen
Karen McCrossan
Marily McGriff
Kathleen McCully
Audrey Misiura
Gerry Moen
Nick Neaton
Jackie Nurnberger
Yvette Oldendorf
Sam Olson
Mary Ostby
Elaine Paumen
Steve Penick
Brent Peterson
Dorothy Peterson
Cindy Redding
Pastor Gale Reitan
Barb Richardson
Robyn Richardson
Dave and Clara Rooney
Nancy Lavender Seeger
Brian Shultz
Mary Smith
Pat Spence
Sally Stevens
Scott Tedrick
Connie Viere
Sharon Vogt
Jim Wagner
Sarah Warmka

Table of Contents

MINNESOTA GHOST TOWNS

Minnesota ghost towns are different. They are not the stuff of Hollywood movie sets nor the iconic "Wild West" images branded into our minds. They don't have the dusty tumble-weed strewn dirt streets lined with weather-beaten buildings. In the Midwest, our ghost towns are more the vanished villages, lost locations, abandoned communities and re-located town sites variety. I call them "places of the past."

In Minnesota, with our abundant natural resources, there are a multitude of these places of the past. Generally based on a one-industry, one-resource economy and the service-oriented support businesses, such as banks, retail stores, saloons, and brothels, the communities thrived as long as the industry or resource did. Once depleted, the industry owners moved to the next location, the supporting businesses failed, the residents moved on and the village faded, leaving few traces of its existence other than perhaps a wide spot along the highway, a clearing in the landscape, a crumbing foundation or two, decrepit weather-beaten buildings, and sometimes a cemetery. Disasters, wars, and changes in the area's economy also contributed to the loss of many towns and communities.

I've long had an interest and personal connection to the notion of ghost towns. My grandparents homesteaded in eastern Montana in a town that would fade into history in the 1920s. My aunt owned land upon which a booming early 1900s Wisconsin logging town was located. The town was abandoned after tornado and fire, leaving few remains.

In the 1970s my mother moved to Hackensack, Minnesota, and lived in a rustic basement cabin on Little Portage Lake. It was my first extended exposure to northern Minnesota, and it took root; I now live here full time and love it more each day.

To get to Mom's place I headed north out of Hackensack, turned west at the intersection of Highway 371 and Cass County #50. Every time we turned at the juncture, Mom would talk of a long-ago town that once sat there. While I had a fleeting fascination, I was young then and hadn't fully developed my love of history. I guess I didn't have enough of my own history to appreciate it as a whole. As years passed, I grew to treasure the past, eventually becoming a history teacher. But back then, I didn't listen as closely as I could have, should have. Not that Mom knew that much about the town, she just knew it used to be there and was intrigued by that fact.

Many years and lots of history have been added to my life since those days. Last year, as I marked a mile-stone birthday, the big sixty, I decided to indulge my interest, pursue my passion and make it my mission to learn all I could, locate, document and visit northern Minnesota's places of the past, those places where lives were lived, children were raised, homes and businesses were created and for various reasons were packed up and moved elsewhere.

This is the story of many of those towns.

WHAT IS A GHOST TOWN?

With no clear-cut definition, determining what constitutes a ghost town is highly subjective, often a matter of degree and opinion.

Purists will define a ghost town—a true ghost town—as a town that has been completely abandoned. Others argue that a ghost town is any community that is a semblance, shadow—or "ghost"—of what it used to be.

At its core, on a basic level, the most agreed upon definition would be that of a human settlement that has been abandoned. With an arbitrary definition in place it is possible to further classify ghost towns into categories or classes based on definitive characteristics.

The most common breakdowns and classes with Minnesota examples are: **

CLASS A – Barren site, nature has reclaimed the land, no visible signs of former inhabitation (Lothrop)

CLASS B – Rubble, foundations, roofless buildings (Gravelville)

CLASS C – Standing abandoned buildings, no/rural population, hamlet, no viable organized community (Gull River)

CLASS D – Semi/Near Ghost town. Many abandoned buildings, small resident population (Lincoln)

CLASS E – Busy historic community—smaller than in boom days (Rose City)

CLASS F – Restored town, historically preserved status (Old Crow Wing – Buena Vista)

A seventh category could also be included:

CLASS G – town joined or was absorbed by neighboring/thriving city (Spina)

Many communities, whatever their class, did leave behind tangible remains in the form of cemeteries. The hallowed grounds are a visible record of the times and lives of the town's inhabitants. Many areas also carry the town's name.

** Modified from Gary Speck's *Classes of Ghost Towns*

LIFE-CYCLE OF A GHOST TOWN

Minnesota, with its abundance of natural resources, has a multitude of used-to-be-towns—ghost towns. Generally based on a one-resource, one-industry economy, the population and all town activity would be heavily dependent on that one factor. The town survived as long as the resource did. Once it was depleted, the industry/owners moved workers and equipment to new locations and new opportunities.

The Michigan Chronoscope E-press describes the process simply and effectively. After the owners/industry moved on, soon the supporting businesses (retail, banks, saloons, brothels, hotels) failed, and the owners closed shop. Residents moved on to new lives, new jobs, homes, and communities. Some towns were dismantled, packed up and shipped out, reassembled in new locations. Others were abandoned and reclaimed by nature. Most left no physical remains except a cemetery or place name.

The earliest settlements first appeared along major transportation routes, primarily rivers. As time would progress, other transportation routes provided prime locations for a town, along tote roads or railroad lines. Others grew in haphazard patterns, when and where there was an opportunity. Native American villages were among the first communities. Though many were seasonal, there were some permanent villages. As settlers moved in, the communities became more permanent.

While each town or community was unique and had its own personality, there was a definite pattern to their life-cycles. The only variable being the rate of progression or pace at which a town moves(ed) through the cycle. Depending on the commodity or resource, this time frame could vary greatly.

Economists, sociologists and historians have labeled this a "boom-and-bust" economy. Models have been created that include definitive characteristics and stages of such an economy. Mining towns, particularly Western mining towns, were the examples most often used in setting the model. In large part, mining towns moved through the progression as a rapid pace. Moving at such an accelerated pace, it was possible to make observations that fit most of the towns that were products of a "boom and bust" economy. Michael Conlin, a business professor in Canada concisely lists the six stages of a "boom and bust" cycle in his book *Mining Heritage and Tourism*. The following are simplified modifications of his model as well as the process described by E-Press:

Stage One – Discovery and Growth
Resource is discovered and developed.
Size of the workforce is capped by workforce required to exploit the resource, often dictated by size and type of resource

Stage Two – Production
Highest level of activity

Stage Three – Decline
Production begins to decline—can be depletion of the resource or a decline in demand.
Can also be that costs have escalated making it unprofitable.
Decline may be rapid.

Stage Four – Abandonment
Owners move equipment and workers to new locations, closing down current production.
Supporting businesses fail/close shop.
Residents move on.

Stage Five – Decay
Town is either packed up or moved on, or buildings are left to decay.

Stage Six – Disappearance of Evidence of Occupation
Everything moved on or reclaimed by nature.

As the E-Press states, towns built on this model were doomed from the beginning to be ghost towns.

LIFE CYCLE BIBLIOGRAPHY

Conlin, Michael V., Lee Joliffe, ed. *Mining Heritage and Tourism: A Global Synthesis.*, UK, Routledge, 2010
"Ghost Towns of Newaygo." E-Press Chronograph Number II. Big Prairie Press. Winter 2007. Web. 16, Nov. 2012

GHOST TOWN CODE OF ETHICS

By their very nature, ghost towns are subject to the ravages of time and the elements. Harsh winter weather and humid summers in Minnesota all take their toll on the remnants of abandoned communities. Vandalism as well as accidental or unintentional damage adds to the deterioration of the sites. It is our duty and responsibility to treat these historic sites with respect and to do all we can to preserve the integrity of ghost towns. Use common sense and follow a code of ethics.

RESPECT PRIVATE PROPERTY.

Many former town sites are now located on private property. Please respect all private property.

Do not trespass—Do not enter private property without permission from the owner.

OBEY ALL POSTED SIGNS

Do not destroy, damage or deface any remains, buildings, or structures.

Do not remove anything from the sites.

Do not cause any disturbance to the foundations, vegetation, or land.

Do not litter. Remove and properly dispose of any trash you take into the area.

Always be courteous, respectful and SAFE.

TREAD LIGHTLY—TAKE ONLY PHOTOS—LEAVE ONLY FOOTPRINTS

Make as little impact on the environment as possible

Honor the past and preserve it for the future.

Anoka County

Cedar in 1909. (Author's collection)

COURTESY
MINNEAPOLIS
STAR

Postcard view of the damage done in the village of Cedar northeast of Anoka. (Author's collection)

CEDAR

1890s - 1993

CLASS G

APPROXIMATE LOCATION:
Presently a neighborhood in Oak Grove

For over forty years, former Marines, including Pat Cooper, searched for the family of Swede Hedlund. In the early days of the Vietnam War they had served with the young man from Minnesota, who they knew only as Swede from Cedar, Minnesota. Swede served as a cook assigned to Company "B" Engineer Platoon. The platoon was stationed in Phu Dai, a remote location in South Vietnam. Swede and his fellow Marines were in a convoy to deliver much needed supplies to an outbase. When one of the convoy drivers was missing, Swede jumped in to drive the truck so that all the vehicles could stay in close contact. The fifteen-mile, enemy-occupied roadway was risky and dangerous, and, as was feared, the convoy was ambushed. Twenty men were killed, with forty more being severely wounded. Swede was one of the soldiers killed.

After the war, several of the Marines began to search for Swede Hedlund's family. They wanted to pay their respects and tell the family of Swede's last hours. Since Swede was Peter Hedlund's nickname and Cedar was an unincorporated location, they had little success finding his family until the Internet helped out. According to an Anoka County Historical Society newsletter and press release, County Commissioner Dennis Berg received a phone call from Pat Cooper, one of the Marines, in 2010.

When Pat Cooper learned that Cedar was in Anoka County, he contacted the first person on the Anoka County website. Commissioner Berg, himself a Vietnam veteran, took it from there. He knew the Hedlund family and put Pat Cooper in touch with Hedlund's siblings. He also organized a Service of Remembrance for Sergeant Hedlund. Over forty people, including the only survivor from the truck convoy that fateful day, gathered at the graveside, sharing tales and tears for the brave young Cedar man.

Cedar, settled by the Irish, lay just west of another used-to-be town, Glen Cary, and was located along Cedar Creek. The area was destroyed by an 1857 prairie fire. However, Cedar developed just after that catastrophe occurred. The community began as a section house on the Great Northern Railroad line from Fridley to Brook Park.

The first store was called the Farmer's Store and served the area's farming population. A blacksmith, an implement dealer, a sorghum mill, several stores, a creamery, a cheese factory, and a Ford garage were also located in the small community. The historic 1939 Anoka tornado destroyed the settlement and several other area locations.

Several community groups were active, including the Grange, Woodmen, and the Cedar Community Club. Supposedly Theodore Roosevelt wrote the club, inquiring about the group's organization, its bylaws, and other details. The Fourth of July celebrations were highlights.

Now some might argue that Cedar still exists, and in a way it does. No longer a town, the entity was officially incorporated into the city of Oak Grove in 1993. The area name, Cedar, now pertains to a neighborhood, rather than the town that once was.

CONSTANCE

1897 - 1974

CLASS G

APPROXIMATE LOCATION:
Absorbed by Andover
Known as Constance Corners - Intersection of County
Roads #18 & 20

When A.O. Johnson became the new postmaster of the new community at the junction of Anoka County 18 and 20, he was given the opportunity to name the settlement. He immediately chose the name Constance for two reasons. The first was in honor of his daughter, the second after the ship *Constantine*, on which he had served as a sailor in his earlier days.

Constance was a stop along the Great Northern Railroad's Elk River to Duluth line. The area had been settled by farmers in the 1860s. By the late 1880s, the village was taking shape. The community's first church, the Constance Free Church, was established in 1893 and was originally built near the cemetery. As membership increased, it was later moved to the corner of Constance Boulevard and County Road #20. When a new church building was constructed in 1981, the original building was moved to the Anoka County Fairgrounds, where it is on display in the Pioneer Village. Church services are conducted during the annual fair run. Weddings and other special events are also hosted in the historic building.

Constance Church 1940s. (Courtesy of Constance Free Church)

Constance Church 1970s. (Courtesy of Constance Free Church)

Constance montage. (Courtesy of Constance Free Church)

A two-room schoolhouse was used from the 1890s until the last graduating class in 1954. The building was later taken down to make room for a turn lane at the intersection. Constance was the community hub, and the baseball field was a gathering place for the entire community. By 1989, the field was filled with weeds and grasshoppers.

The Constance Grange was established in 1935 with twenty-five members. The organization promoted education and fostered community improvement projects. Declining membership dissolved the group.

Constance began to decline in the 1950s. The store and post office closed. Postal services were transferred to the Anoka Post Office. With the completion of Highway 65, it was easier to travel to larger communities to shop, where there was more variety and less expensive prices.

In 1974, the Grow Town Board elected to incorporate with the City of Andover under the name of Andover. The name Andover has a fun folk-lore name legend. It is said that when

Constance School. (Courtesy of Constance Free Church)

one of the first trains to travel on the Great Northern tracks during the 1890s tipped over in a swamp in the southeast section of the township, one of the witnesses reported that the train "went over and over and over." Thus Andover.

Today, the area is bustling and busy. The Constance Free Church still stands and is active and vibrant. The name lives on in the area, giving testament to the fact that Constance was also once a busy, thriving community and, in ways, still is.

4

GLEN CARY

1856 - 1857

CLASS A/G

APPROXIMATE LOCATION:
Absorbed by Ham Lake

Early Scandinavian farmers, who had settled in the area as early as 1856, built a Lutheran Church, as well as a few rudimentary homes and called the area Glen Cary, meaning "beautiful valley." Located in Grow Township, the town was platted in 1857. That same year a prairie fire destroyed everything. Little was rebuilt except for the church. An argument ensued over the official language of the church services, Swedish or Norwegian. The devisive issue split the congregation in two, with each building their own church. The Swedish built the Swedish Evangelical Church and the Norwegians built Glen Cary Lutheran Church. Grow Township was absorbed by area communities and became known as Ham Lake. Both churches are still active and both claim to be the original and oldest church in the area.

JOHNSVILLE

1893 - 1970s

CLASS G

APPROXIMATE LOCATION:
Highway 65 & Anoka County #14

It must have had quite an impact on me as, nearly fifty-fife years later, I can remember Johnsville, primarily for the meat market. Although memories sometime remain fuzzy, I clearly remember the plate-glass window in the meat locker where shoppers, visitors, and even school children on field trips could watch the cattle being loaded into the chutes and be prepared for the processing. My mind's eyes can see the cows being huddled into stalls. When we finished watching, we would go buy our meats.

Johnsonville was established in 1893 around the school. Area farmers built a school for grades one through five. The site selected was an equal distance from most of the homes of the area's schoolchildren. Central Avenue during the 1920s was already a major thoroughfare. John Auguston and Henry Trost built a garage and grocery store along the busy roadway. A 1925 storm (tornado) destroyed the businesses, the school, and several homes. Auguston rebuilt his store and urged others to build in the vicinity as well. In honor of Auguston's unfailing support, residents called the community Johnsville. Though the town itself is now gone, the neighborhood and the name survive. An area school, library, and several other locations use the Johnsville name.

SODERVILLE

1920s - 1980s

CLASS G

APPROXIMATE LOCATION:
Absorbed by Ham Lake

Despite being destroyed by a cyclone the week before it was set to open, the Soderville Store was rebuilt and opened in 1926. The store joined the small community located around Central Avenue. The Central Garage was next to the store and was so named because it was halfway between Minneapolis and Cambridge. Business was brisk and soon the garage started selling auto accessories, even motor vehicle licenses. A Chevrolet dealership was also established. The garage had a local Greyhound Bus depot. Later other businesses joined the community and included a hamburger and root beer stand. The business was owned by two Soderquist brothers.

The store, owned and operated by two other Soderquist brothers was doing a thriving business as well. Offering a wide variety of goods, the barter system was an option for area farmers. A full-service store, people would take their lists into the store, and clerks would run through the store picking up the items. Every order received a free bag of candy.

Recreational opportunities were many and included a Salvation Army Band. Outdoor movies were always popular as were baseball and hockey. Baseball, the most popular, sometimes hosted over 1,000 spectators, far outdistancing the town's population.

Central Avenue became Highway 65. In 1958, when the highway was enlarged to four lanes, the east side of Soderville was lost to the expansion. The South Bound lane of Highway 65 is where the original store stood. In 1989, the Soderquist Super Valu was in the area. The name lives on, not as a town, but as a neighborhood. It seems the Soderquist brothers knew a good location when they saw it.

Soderville then and now (postcard—late 1990s). (Author's Collection)

Benton County

Above: Brennyville store, 2014. (Author's Collection) Below: Brennyville store today. (Author's Collection)

BRENNYVILLE

1923 – 1950s

CLASS D

APPROXIMATE LOCATION:
Benton County Road 14 and 165th Street NE

Founding the St. Elizabeth Catholic Church in 1923, Father Peter Brenny not only cared for his parishioners' spiritual guidance and needs, he also did all he could to provide for their worldly well-being as well.

The forty-five families living in the area at the time were primarily dairy farmers. In 1924, Father Brenny established a store with an "L" addition. The store and "L," both two stories, were quite large for the time, the store being forty by one hundred feet and the addition forty-six by seventy-two feet. Living quarters were in the back.

To provide an outlet for the area farmers' dairy products, Father Brenny launched a cheese factory in 1928. Hiring a cheese factory manager from Wisconsin, the Father also purchased a truck to haul the cheese to Wisconsin, where it was marketed. Farmers brought their milk to the factory where it was made into several varieties of cheese. Most were made into twenty-five-pound cheese rounds, although some smaller bricks were made. The Brennyville community hosted parish festivals and dinners, dances, weddings, receptions, and community plays. Most events were held in the store.

In the 1940s, during church services, the store caught fire, supposedly from a blow torch that exploded. Within minutes the building was engulfed in flames, reaching as high as 125 feet into the air. Damages were estimated at $35,000. Deciding not to rebuild, parishoners purchased a thirty-four-by-eighty-foot building across the street from the store and moved it onto the former store's foundation. The building was used as a hall and community center as well as a small store.

The original St. Elizabeth Church operated until 1951, when a new church was built. That church still stands and is

Brennyville today. (Author's Collection)

St. Elilzabeth's Catholic Church, Brennyville, today. (Author's Collection)

9

very active. Even though Father Brenny was transferred to other parishes, he was buried in the St. Elizabeth Cemetery upon his death in 1955.

St. Elizabeth's is a majestic as ever and is a local landmark. The small store building still stands and the "Brennyville Store" sign, though faded, can be read. The store building is being made into a private home. A few other homes are in the area.

FRUITVILLE (FRUTHVILLE)

1901 – 1950s

CLASS A

APPROXIMATE LOCATION:
Crossroads of Benton County Roads #1 & #13
NW of Foley, ½ mile East of Mayhew Lake

Got milk? The popular advertising phrase could apply to Benton County's community of Fruitville as well. Built on the creamery, sustained by the creamery and done in (partially) by the World War II milk routes, Fruitville's existence was dictated by the rise and fall of the dairy business.

Back in 1901, Peter Fruith bought five acres of land. He soon built a general store, blacksmith shop and a creamery. He ran the businesses for twenty years; later it operated as a coop. Sometime between 1939 and 1944, the creamery and adjoining ice house were closed and torn down. During World War II, milk routes were begun and, though very popular, they significantly hurt the rural creameries, causing many of them to close. As creameries went so did some communities.

An alternate or contributing factor to Fruitville's demise was the decision to build the new Catholic Church in Mayhew Lake instead of Fruitville.

There was great debate and controversy on where to build the new church. Arguments from both sides touted the advantages of one community while emphasizing the disadvantages of the other. Proponents of locating the church in Fruitville said that putting the church in Mayhew Lake would put the church at the extreme western edge of the community, which was an area with few families. Those supporting the Mayhew Lake location said Fruitville was too swampy and wet,

Fruithville Store. (Benton County Historical Society)

plus it was too close to the Catholic Church in Gilman. The hierarchy of the Catholic diocese, without listening to any input from interested parties, decided on the Mayhew Lake location.

Another important component of Fruitville was the Fruitville Store. Said to carry a bit of everything a farm home could need, the store was at the heart of the community and the quintesential convenience store of the past. It carried everything (except for bread and canned goods, as farm families made their own) from flour, sugar, candy, shotgun shells, shoes, shirts, cloth, and more. According to record, there was one clerk at the store, known for her penny pinching ways. She weighed the candy, and if it was overweight, she would bite a piece of the candy off and put the remainder back in the bag.

When the store got its first radio in the 1920s, the area children marveled at the skills used in operating the new invention. Operating under several owners, the store later became a tavern. The owners finally tired of the long hours needed to run the tavern, so in the 1950s, they closed it, tore it down and moved to St. Cloud.

In 2006, *The St. Cloud Times*, did a feature article on Larry and Leon Hasbch, sons of an early storekeeper. The brothers, in their seventies, would travel back to Fruitville, in person and in memories. They were saddened by the demise of the town. No longer physically existing, the town lives on in the hearts and minds of many.

LANGOLA

1857 - 1878

CLASS A

APPROXIMATE LOCATION:
2 miles south of Royalton (County 40)
At the present site of the bridge over the Platte River

Normally serene and tranquil, Central Minnesota's Platte River could, at times, become a raging torrent. The residents of Benton County's Langola were well aware of the river's moods. On flat land just a few feet above the river, the town was favorably situated. Originally called Platte River, the post office for Langola actually began as Royalton in 1854. In 1858 the post office was transferred to Langola where it operated until 1878 when services were transferred to Royalton. According to Warren Upham's *Minnesota Place Names*, Langola is uniquely named, meaning the name does not appearing anywhere else.

Serving as a stop on the stage coach route, coaches would

stop twice a week, and tired teams of horses were fed and watered. For several years the town was prosperous. A flour mill, two hotels, a school, two saloons, a sawmill, other stores, a trading post, a blacksmith, and other establishments provided all the services the residents could want or need. There was even a newspaper, *The Frontier*, the first paper to be published outside of St. Paul and St. Anthony, for a few years.

Situated on both sides of the river, a bridge provided necessary access. Over the years floods did damage to the bridge, which was always repaired, until the year when the river raged, destroying the dam and washing the town away except for one residence. That home was built on higher ground. Shortly after the flood, the remaining home's owner moved the house south to a new location on the Mississippi River. After the disastrous flood, the town was not rebuilt and was deserted by 1879. Today a new bridge over the Platte River marks the old town site.

MEDORA

1850s

CLASS A

APPROXIMATE LOCATION:
Southwest of present day Gilman
4 miles north of Popple Creek

Hoping not only to stake out their homesteads, the newly arrived settlers planned to purchase extra land to sell to subsequent newcomers to the area. In addition, reaping the area's vast timber resources was an added bonus and incentive. The community of Medora (not listed in Upham's *Minnesota Place Names* or in postal history resources) was 320 acres in area and was platted in the mid-1850s. The plat had the streets all laid out, named and numbered. Things, however did not go as planned.

Edward Sowa, an area historian, noted that the region was far off the beaten path and very swampy. Transportation was poor. There were no permanent settlers in the area, although there were a few shelters and cabins. After two years, everyone, even the town's promoters left.

Several years later, settlers did start coming to the region. Primarily interested in farming, the nearby river provided needed water sources. This too was short-lived and the land has reverted back to nature.

POPPLE CREEK

1896 – 2000s

CLASS D

APPROXIMATE LOCATION:
Golden Spike Road and 65th Avenue NE

Boys will be boys, and it doesn't seem to matter if it is in today's world or decades ago. Back in the early 1900s, St. John's Evangelical Lutheran Church sat next to the Popple Creek store. Church officials were not happy with the fact that the store was open during church services. At the least it was distracting, it was also quite the temptation for the younger members of the congregation, who would, at times, sneak out of the balcony and head over to the store, sneaking

Popple Creek Store. (Benton County Historical Society)

Popple Creek Store today. (Benton County Historical Society)

back into the church before services ended. As area historian Edward Sowa tells, one Sunday the deacons instructed the front doors to be locked after services began. Sure enough, just before the service ended, a group of young folks were caught standing on the church steps, barred from their entry back to the balcony, their clever plan foiled.

First called Raether, the community was named for a German immigrant, store and saloon owner and the first postmaster. The post office was only in existence for a few years and only under the name of Raether. The earliest settlers were from Masuren Prussia, an enclave near the Polish border. They settled in Minnesota as it looked very much like their homeland. The church and store were the mainstays of the town, which also included a blacksmith and potato warehouse.

In 1909 the store burned but was quickly replaced with a two-story building. There were living quarters in the back and a dance hall on the upper floor. The dance hall was also used for weddings, community meetings, and other social events. A succession of owners operated the store, and, at one point, it was turned into a tavern with a pool table, grilled food, and a few grocery staples. It operated until the late twentieth century.

SILVER CORNERS

1920s - Present?

CLASS C

APPROXIMATE LOCATION:
Intersection of Benton County 2 and Highway 25

Painted silver, the store gave the crossroads community its name. Built in 1922 by Joe Skaya, the store/tavern has operated many years as does the nearby Silver Corner Storage.

Silver Corners store. (Benton County Historical Society)

Silver Corners store today. (Author's collection)

Former Watab School and Town Hall. (Courtesy of the Watab Town Board/Pat Spence)

WATAB

1852 – 1885

1891 – 1914

CLASS A

APPROXIMATE LOCATION:
Two miles north of present day Sartell, NW corner of Section 34

There are few areas in Central Minnesota as historically significant as the lost town of Watab and its surrounding area. Named for the long slender roots of the jackpine and tamarack trees, the roots were used as threads in the making of canoes and wigwams.

Famed explorer Zebulon Pike was in the region in 1805. Writing in his journal, he described the difficulties he and his crew experienced in getting their large wooden boats over the Sauk and Watab rapids. It took six days to travel from Sauk Rapids to a spot between Royalton and Little Falls. The Benton County Historical Society writes that the Watab Rapids were submerged in later years, when a dam was constructed at Sartell.

Also important in Native American history, Chief Watab built his camp near Little Rock Lake. Nearby is an outcropping of granite that marked the boundary between the Ojibwe and Dakota as set in the 1825 treaty. Henry Schoolcraft, in 1832, gave the granite boulder the name "Peace Rock."

Watab experienced its greatest growth in the mid-nineteenth century. Located on the Red River Oxcarts Woods Trail, the community was considered the most important commercial site northwest of St. Paul. The American Fur Company operated a trading post in 1848. That year also saw David Gilman purchasing a farm (Benton County's first) and building a hotel. Soon a store and bakery were built near the hotel.

Platted and surveyed in 1854, the next few years saw continued growth. A bridge, the first upriver from St. Anthony, was built in 1856. Shortly after construction, strong winds caused the bridge to collapse. It was repaired and rebuilt.

Nathan Myrick opened a general store. Nathan's brother, Andrew Myrick, is a name infamous in Minnesota history. Andrew was the agent who, when faced with the starving Dakotas' pleas for their promised supplies and annuities, spoke the words, "Let them eat grass." That statement is considered the spark that ignited the Dakota Conflict of 1862. Andrew Myrick was later found dead, with grass stuffed in his mouth.

After Nathan Myrick's store, other retail services would join the community.

One resource referenced a Watab gold and silver mine. A long-time resident said it provided enough gold to make one ring.

A post office was established in 1856, and Watab was designated the Benton County seat. Records indicate that Watab truly prospered only during the time it served as the county seat. When the county seat and courthouse were moved to Sauk Rapids, businesses left, and the town declined, eventually fading into history. The yellow-brick Watab school closed in 1946 when enrollment declined to five students. The building later served as the Watab Town Hall until a new building was constructed in 2006. Later Foley would become the county seat.

WILLIAMSVILLE

1873 - 1877

CLASS A

APPROXIMATE LOCATION:
¾ mile south of Gilman, on West side of Golden Spike Road

Largely unknown, even people who grew up in the area had never heard of Williamsville. Edward Sowa, area historian, extensively researched the community. Listed only on early government maps and in limited resources, Williamsville appears to have been the center of commerce for the region. Records indicate the town consisted of a hotel, restaurant, post office and general store. Sowa also notes that the region had abundant wildlife. From September 1873 until January of 1874, nearly 40,000 pounds of venison was harvested for market. Cheese, butter, granite, flour, and cranberries were also shipped in abundance to Eastern U.S. markets.

Big Stone County

Early Artichoke Lake settlers. (Courtesy of Kathryn Draeger)

Artichoke Store 1936-1937. (Courtesy of Big Stone County Historical Society)

Artichoke Lake Store Today (notice 8-sided building in background). (Courtesy of Larry Helgeson)

ARTICHOKE LAKE

1876 - 1913

CLASS C

APPROXIMATE LOCATION:
9.7 miles west/northwest of Appleton on T-146

Early settlers, many from Norway, often lived their first year in dugouts or sod houses. Many Native Americans also lived in the region, and tepees along the lake were a common sight. Breaking ground for those early white settlers and making a life was hard, strenuous work. The first crops were wheat and rutabagas. Weather was always a factor in their tenuous lives, regardless of the season. Since family and friends were often great distances apart, one of the most important services a community could offer was mail delivery. Nearly every settlement, every town, and community, regardless of size, petitioned for designation as a post office. In the late 1880s, Big Stone County had twenty post offices. By comparison, today there are eight.

One of the earliest mail routes in the county was in the community of Artichoke Lake. The name Artichoke Lake was translated from the Sioux for "the edible tubular roots of a species of sunflowers," which grew in abundance in the area. Citizens took mail delivery seriously. According to the Big Stone County Historical Society, Nicaus Nelson drove one of the earliest routes, traveling the twenty-mile one-way distance to Ortonville and then back again on rudimentary roads that were often a challenge.

Prepared for any inclement weather, Nicaus used a light wagon with an enclosure to help protect him from the elements. Every Minnesotan knows weather in the state can change in a moment, sunshine quickly shifting to overcast, fine weather become foul without much preamble. In the winter time, storms could develop and turn dangerous in just a short time, certainly in the space of time it took Nicaus to drive his route. One such snow storm caught Nicaus by surprise. As Big Stone County Historical Society records state, "The storm very quickly reached blizzard proportions, and Nicaus could not see a thing, not even the horses in front of him. Realizing he could not steer the horses, he let them go on their own. After what seemed to be a very long time, the horses stopped in their tracks. Getting out to investigate, Nicaus learned that the horse's heads had hit the wall of his home. Unable to even see the light placed in the window as a guide, the horses had led him home."

Covering a wide geographic area throughout the township, the town of Artichoke Lake was an active and very social community and occupied about forty acres. The octagon school, though part of the community was approximately four miles from the "town" hub. A town band, with twenty-two members, purchased the old school building and held weekly practices. The second town band operated from 1916 to 1933. A Sailor's Club was active in the 1890s. The area had several churches, including Baptist and Lutheran denominations. A creamery built in 1906 made butter, some of which was shipped to outlets as far away as New York.

The Artichoke Lake Store was operated by a succession of owners and located in several buildings within the community. The 1930s era building still survives and is now located on the grounds of the Big Stone County Historical Society's Museum in Ortonville. No longer stocking the staples and goods needed by the community's residents, the store currently houses the Charles Hanson North American Wildlife Collection that includes waterfowl, birds of prey, and rare birds whose habitat ranges from Alaska to Mexico. According to the Historical Society's brochure and the *Minneapolis StarTribune* it is considered one of the largest and most impressive collections in the United States and quite possibly the world.

Also included on the museum grounds is an eight-sided school house. The school operated in Artichoke Lake from 1898 to 1955. It is now listed on the National Register of Historic Places.

Artichoke Lake Baptist Church. (Robin Johnson)

(Courtesy of the Carver County Historical Society)

Carver County

Assumption store (above). (Courtesy of A. Filer)

Assumption today (at left). (Courtesy of A. Filer)

Benton. (Author's collection)

East Union. (Courtesy of A. Filer)

ASSUMPTION

1881 - 1906

CLASS C

APPROXIMATE LOCATION:
Eight miles Northeast of Green Isle, 180th Street and County Highway 33

Little is known about the small community named for the settlement's Catholic Church.

BENTON

1850s - 1900

CLASS A

APPROXIMATE LOCATION:
One-half mile north of Cologne, northeast shore of Lake Benton

First settled in the mid 1850s, the town of Benton was not platted until 1880. The community named for U.S. Senator Thomas Hart Benton had a post office from 1861 until 1880. Little else is known about the community.

BONGARD

1876 - 1972

CLASS A/G

APPROXIMATE LOCATION:
County Highway #15, one mile south of Highway #212

Oftentimes a community's creamery outlasted the community itself. Nowhere else is that more true than in Bongard, Minnesota. In fact, Bongard has now become synonymous with cheese, and the creamery has become the historic face of the early Carver County community. While there is little documentation on the town itself, the history of the creamery is well-documented.

Bongard, the town, was located on the Soo Line Railroad and was in the heart of farm country. The community had a grain elevator, feed mill and a few necessary businesses. A post office operated at times from 1872 until 1976.

In 1908, area farmers formed the Bongard's Cooperative Creamery. Thirty years later, in 1938, the equipment and technology had become outdated. Many small communities chose to dissolve their creameries in these instances rather than spend the money to update them. But not so Bongard's. That community chose to make the necessary and expensive upgrades and have continued to do so throughout the years as techology changed and equipment aged. Now an industry leader, Bongard's is the finest cheese available anywhere. Still located in the historic community, Bongard's has also expanded to other areas of the state. The community still has many original buildings still standing.

EAST UNION

1853 - 1903

CLASS D

APPROXIMATE LOCATION:
Bordering Dahlgren and San Francisco Townships, County Roads #40 and #50, nearby East Union Elementary School

Settled in 1853 by Swedish immigrants, the community of East Union was first known as Bevers Creek and as Oscar's Settlement in honor of Oscar the First, then king of Sweden and Norway. In 1858, a Swedish Lutheran Congregation was formed with 100 families. Later the community developed into two sections, one part being called East Union. A post office there operated from 1873 until 1903. The community also included a cooperative creamery, a sorghum mill, and a grist mill. Little is known about the demise of the community.

East Union. (Courtesy of A. Filer)

GOTHA

1884 – 1910s

CLASS C

APPROXIMATE LOCATION:
Boundary between Benton and Hancock Townships, near intersection of County Highways # 53 and # 50

Gotha building. (Courtesy of A. Filer)

Named for the ancient central German city of Gotha, Gotha, Minnesota, is located at the border of Benton and Hancock townships in Carver County. The small community had a general store, a creamery, and a windmill factory. A post office operated from 1884 to 1902. Little else is known about the community.

Gotha today. (Courtesy of A. Filer)

Gotha scene today. (Courtesy of A. Filer)

HAZELTON

EARLY 1900s

CLASS A

APPROXIMATE LOCATION:
Five miles north of New Germany, along Luce Line Trail
between Watertown and Winsted

Occupying a small parcel of land, just one-half mile wide, the community of Hazelton was home to a lumberyard, a feed mill/elevator, a general store, creamery, ice house (ice was cut from nearby Lake Ida), and the train depot. The store was located a mile from the depot.

During the day, train passengers could purchase their tickets at the store. Night time passengers had to light a rolled newspaper to flag the train down. Once boarded they could buy their tickets.

The Electric Short Line Railroad came through the area in 1908. The Murphy family sold fifty feet of their property with the stipulation that the station be named after their daughter,

Hazel. Thus, Hazelton it became. With a small population, as families moved from the area, the community shrank proportionally. In 1970, the Luce Line was abandoned, the tracks pulled up and covered with crushed limestone. It is now a recreational trail. A historic sign has been placed at the old town site and some foundations can still be seen.

HELVETIA

1856 - 1888

CLASS A/G

APPROXIMATE LOCATION:
Southeast corner of Hollywood Township

Using the ancient name for Switzerland, Helvetia was located near Mayer. A diphtheria epidemic swept through the community in its early years. Later, when Mayer got railroad service and Helvetia didn't, all activity moved to Mayer. The post office was transferred as well.

Early Helvetia. (Courtesy of the Carver County Historical Society)

SAN FRANCISCO

1856 - 1862

CLASS C

APPROXIMATE LOCATION:
San Francisco Township, near Jordan

When he arrived in Carver County from the West Coast, William Foster named his newly established townsite, San Francisco. Having friends in high places, Foster used his influence to secure a post office and county seat designation for the town as well.

San Francisco's location along the Minnesota River was not ideal; in fact, it was far from it. The river flooded every year, and the nearby rapids made it difficult for steamboats, or any other vessels, to reach the small community. Even so, Foster built a store and warehouse in 1857. A ferry began operating in 1859, and a school was established in 1857. In 1858 a meeting formally declared San Francisco a town, and town officials were elected.

Keeping the county seat designation for just a year, its loss played a major role in the demise of the town. Two larger communities downstream, Carver and Chaska, both rapidly expanding and with growing populations, eroded San Francisco's base. A major flood in 1860 destroyed most of San Francisco's buildings and was seemingly the last straw. Most residents and the remaining businesses moved to other area communities.

Hillstrom House. (Courtesy of Carver County Historical Society)

24

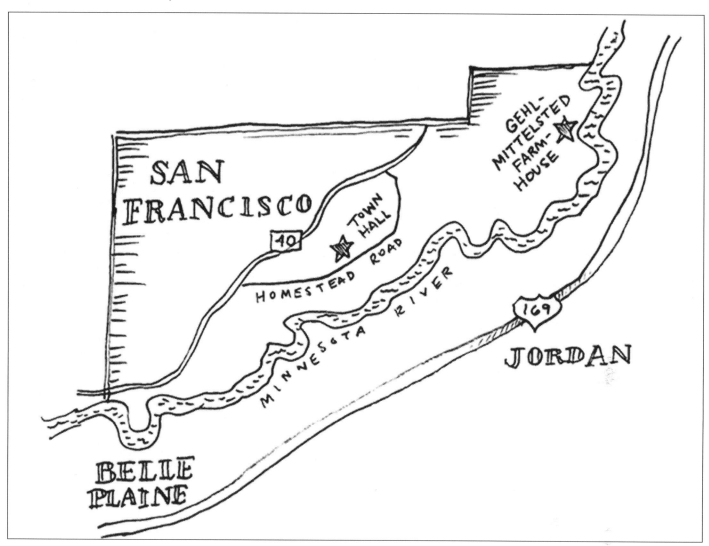

Map of San Francisco. (Courtesy of Andy Sturdevant)

San Francisco Remnants. (Courtesy of Andy Sturdevant)

San Francisco Today . (Courtesy of Andy Sturdevant)

SWEDE LAKE

?

CLASS A

APPROXIMATE LOCATION:
Just south and east of Watertown

For quite a while Swede Lake and Watertown knew nothing of each other's existence. Tales tell that one night a Swede Lake resident got lost and ended up in Watertown. When he got home, he told his neighbors about the nearby town. Before long, the residents of both towns knew each other very well. As Watertown became the trade center, Swede Lake moved to Watertown, merging the two communities into one.

Chippewa County

Street view, Historic Chippewa City. (Courtesy of the Chippewa County Historical Society)

Gazebo view, Historic Chippewa City. (Courtesy of the Chippewa County Historical Society)

CHIPPEWA CITY

1868 - 1870

CLASS A/G

APPROXIMATE LOCATION:
Now part of Montevideo, Smith's Addition

Not willing to take no for an answer, a small group of men from Montevideo decided they had to do something. Representatives from the newly established community of Montevideo on the east side of the Chippewa River went to the Minnesota Legislature and asked to be made the county seat. Chippewa City, the senior community by two years, also on the banks of the river, already held the county seat designation, but it was a smaller community than Montevideo. The legislature replied that Chippewa City was there first, and, since they had the mail route and, more importantly, the post office, they would remain the county seat.

Taking matters into their own hands, the men, in the middle of the night, rowed a boat across the river and stole the post office, which at that time was just a box. Once they had the post office safely secured in their town, they went back to St. Paul and told the legislature they now had the post office. Without any questions, Montevideo was immediately made the temporary county seat and shortly thereafter the permanent seat.

Chippewa City, the county's first community, fell into decline. With time it became part of Montevideo in a neighborhood known as Smith's Addition.

Historic Chippewa City street scene. (Courtesy of the Chippewa County Historical Society)

Horse power event, Historic Chippewa City. (Courtesy of the Chippewa County Historical Society)

HISTORIC CHIPPEWA CITY

Though we are no longer able to physically walk the streets of Chippewa City, the Chippewa County Historical Society, with vision, dedication, and hard work, has preserved the essence and spirit of the late 1800s town, allowing us to step back in time and experience history first-hand.

Historic Chippewa City began in 1965 with the preservation of a rural school house. In 1967 John Swennson donated his father, Ole's, original farmstead. The seventeen-acre site included an 1880s timber-frame barn, remains of the grist mill, the family cemetery and the twenty-two-room brick farmhouse. Over the years, several buildings have been moved into the historic compound. Still others were built on-site to complement the recreated community. At present, there are twenty-four buildings, each furnished with authentic artifacts, and the Anderson Cabin is said to be one of the most authentically furnished log cabins in all of Minnesota.

According to the Chippewa County Historical Society brochure and website, the buildings include:

Millinery and Dress Shop	Print Shop
Law Office	Fire Department
Brown's Brothers Fuel and Ice	Buggy Shop

Post Office (formerly the Reasor Post Office [now a lost town] previously located three miles East of Watson. It was built in 1870 and served the area until 1880 when a post office was established in Watson)

Chippewa Bank	Bath and Shine
Harness Shop	Blacksmith
Ness House	Anderson Log Cabin
School House	Village Church
Church Museum	Dr. Burns' Office
Village Hall	Burns Fur Trading Post
Gazebo	

Anderson cabin, Historic Chippewa City. (Courtesy of the Chippewa County Historical Society)

Historic Chippewa City School. (Courtesy of the Chippewa County Historical Society)

All the historic original buildings were in use in Chippewa County in the late 1880s to the early 1900s.

Also on the grounds is the Gateway Building, which is the home of the Chippewa County Historical Society, a research center/library, with rest rooms (modern day).

The historic village is open from Memorial Day to Labor Day, and Monday through Friday throughout September.

Special events hosted annually include:

Horse Power Event: the second Saturday of September, horse-drawn power, demonstrations in plowing, cultivating, crafts and artisans, rug making, and many other activities.

Christmas in the Village: the first Saturday of December, there is a different theme each year and includes horse-drawn rides, Santa Claus, crafts, foods and more.

Heritage Week: second week of May, open to school children only.

Mission Sunday: second Sunday in July, at the Lac Qui Parle Mission.

Christmas in Historic Chippewa City. (Courtesy of the Chippewa County Historical Society)

HAGAN

1869 – 1910'S

CLASS C

APPROXIMATE LOCATION:
12 Miles Southeast of Appleton on Highway #9 just north of Highway 11

Hagan farmstead. (Courtesy of A. Filer)

Little is written about Hagen. Settled in 1869, a post office was established in 1872 and operated until 1907. For a short time the post office was transferred to Swift County (1881 to 1883) and then returned to Chippewa County until 1907. The community was named for early settler N.K. Hagen. The post office misspelled his name on the official records and wasn't corrected. Records state that the community had a population of thirty-three in 1895 and that no rail service was at the community, which most likely caused its decline and demise.

Hagan today. (Courtesy of A. Filer)

Chisago County

Buildings in Franconia. (Courtesy of the Franconia Town Board)

DANEWOOD

1870 - 1902

CLASS A

APPROXIMATE LOCATION:
Nessel Township

In the early days of Danewood, with only Native American trails to follow, getting supplies and groceries was a chore. Settlers had to walk the crude trails to Rush City to get groceries and if they needed flour, to Sunrise. Then came the hard part, they had to carry the goods back home and a sack of flour weighed 100 pounds. Often two men made the trip together they could take turns carrying the heavy load. The trip took two days in good conditions. The swampy terrain made the journey difficult even in the best of weather.

Danewood was settled by Danish immigrants as the name suggests. The name originated with the settlers' nationality plus the setting in the heavily wooded area, thus Danewood. It was also the first Danish settlement on the Minnesota map.

A sawmill was in the area as early as 1870. In 1882 a post office was established, which was discontinued in 1902. The town also included a blacksmith, who made steel plows, a church, two creameries, and a general store.

FRANCONIA

1858 - 1900

CLASS A

APPROXIMATE LOCATION:
St. Lawrence Creek on the west and the St. Croix River on the west, Highway 95 two miles south of Taylors Falls

Filled with strange and unusual critters and objects, today's Franconia is filled with eclectic and creative sculptures. More on that later.

Before locating to Franconia, early settler Ansel Smith helped build the Chisago Hotel, the landmark hotel that has served the area since 1851. In 1852, Smith moved two miles

Franconia Buildings (Opposite). (Courtesy of Franconia Town Hall)

Franconia Sculpture Park. (Courtesy of Franconia Sculpture Park)

south of Taylors Falls to the area he called Franconia. The site, located between the St. Lawrence Creek on the west and the St. Croix River on the east, was from the beginning, a lumber and river town. Many say timber made the town, and timber, or the absence of it, was its end. Certainly water power and river access made the town location seeming ideal. Possessing water power for mills, a safe boat landing, a gentle slope to the river and a firm sand shore all helped in the development of the town's industries and its growth.

Two versions explain the naming of Franconia. The first has it that Smith, a teacher in St. Croix Falls, named the site for his hometown in the White Mountains of New Hampshire. The other version says the village and the township were named for Smith's son, Francis, who died shortly before Smith arrived in Minnesota.

Franconia Sawmill and Lumberyard. (Courtesy of Franconia Town Board)

Franconia today. (Courtesy of Franconia Sculpture Park)

In 1852 development began with the construction of homes along the St. Lawrence Creek. Smith added a "lean to" onto his small cabin and began a trading post. That same year, two Day brothers began a factory, making wood plugs that were used in the construction of log rafts. The plugs gave the town its nickname "Plugtown." Soon a sawmill and stave mill were operating "full steam" in the quickly growing settlement. The sawmill was large and the equipment powerful. The circular saw was powered by a forty-horse-power engine. It is said that the first white pine cut on the St. Croix was cut at Franconia.

In 1861 a steamboat-building facility was up and running. Several ships, including the *Jenny Thornton*, the *Ben Campbell* and more were built on the sandy shores of the St. Croix River as were river barges. A second sawmill was added in 1870 and this one employed twelve men. At its peak, Franconia had a population of 500 and the town was a bustling community with two hotels, two stores, two schools, two blacksmiths, three saloons, a post office operating from 1866 to 1898, a restaurant, confectionary, doctor, gunsmith, and the above building factories.

The first school classes were held in the bar of one of the hotels. Ten students were enrolled. A designated school was built in 1870.

Routing through the area in 1878, the St. Paul & Dakota Railroad build the Franconia depot one mile from the town. By that time the timber recourses were quickly becoming depleted. River traffic was on the decline as well, and soon Franconia would disappear. As with most communities of the time, businesses and residents would pack up and move on.

Two Franconia men are credited with the development of the famed Haralson apple. Fred Haralson had a nursery on Highway 8 just west of Highway 95. Fred and his brother, from Sweden were employed as horticulturists at the University of Minnesota Excelsior based farm. Fred eventually became the farm's superintendent. The Haralsons, called their new apple Number 90. They had open pollinated the seed for the Malinda apple, which had been planted in 1908 and was hardy enough to survive the harsh winter of 1917/1918. Carefully caring for the trees, the first fruit came in 1913 and was released for public sale in 1922 with the name of Haralson.

Back to the surreal sculptures in today's Franconia. Franconia Sculpture Park is an artist residency and non-profit arts organization. The twenty-five-acre site is open to the public and showcases over 105 large scale sculptures. People of all ages can take the self-guided tours; even dogs on leashes are welcome. The self-guided tours are free and open 365 days a year from dawn to dusk. The park also offers a full line of activities for all ages. Each sculpture has an information sign telling what it is, who made it and more. People may even come upon visiting artists and get a chance to talk to them about their art in progress.

KOST

1883 - 1904

CLASS A

APPROXIMATE LOCATION:
Sunrise Township

Settled on both sides of the Sunrise River, available water power attracted the first settlers. Founder F.A. Kost, for whom the town was named, built a dam and set up a mill and post office in 1883. At its height, Kost had a sawmill, flour mill, feed mill, post office, general store, blacksmith, school, and a creamery. Kost was farm country, and potatoes were the cash crop. Though little remains of the community, the church is still active today.

Kost Street Scene, May 29, 1912. (Shawn Hewitt Collection)

PALMDALE

1899 - 1903

CLASS C

APPROXIMATE LOCATION:
Corner of Highway 95 and County Highway 71

I have driven by Palmdale and noticed the old store standing in the quiet farmland setting. Usually a quiet farming community it was said that, on Saturday nights, Palmdale would come to life when the dance hall had a jazz band, dancing, and 190-proof moonshine mixed with grape soda.

In addition to the dance hall, the town, in 1900, had a store, creamery, blacksmith, and a post office for a short time. Never having their own church, residents attended church services in nearby Almelund and Taylors Falls. The old store, no longer in business, marks the town site as does a green highway marker.

PANOLA

1865 - 1901

CLASS A

APPROXIMATE LOCATION:
Chisago Lake Township

When the first German settlers arrived in the area in 1865 they called the area Prairie Hollow. The name, lasting nearly twenty-five years was changed when a country post office was established in 1899. The post office was discontinued in 1901. The small community had a skimming station (which separated the cream from the milk), a school, a brickyard, and a lodge house. There was also a nearby sawmill.

Richard Widmark Birthplace, Sunrise. (Author's collection)

RUSH POINT

1879 - 1903

CLASS A/G

APPROXIMATE LOCATION:
Now part of Rush City

Rush Point had the usual list of businesses and services, a steam sawmill, several churches, a general store, a blacksmith, a post office (from 1879 to 1903), a tavern, and one business not so common in early towns, a bowling alley. The community was absorbed by Rush City in the early 1900s.

STARK

1868/1904

CLASS A

APPROXIMATE LOCATION:
Fish Lake Township

Stark's first store opened as early as 1867, and a post office was established that year as well. At one time the town included three stores. Named for early settler Lars Stark, the community was rather short-lived, and there are no remains.

SUNRISE

1856 - 1954

CLASS A

APPROXIMATE LOCATION:
County Road 9 (Sunrise Road) and River Road

Had a few votes been swayed, one way or the other, Sunrise might have been the birthplace of a U.S. president. As it turned out, the delegates to the 1920 Republican Convention were deadlocked. No candidate was able to gain the winning percentage. So a compromise was reached and Warren G. Harding won the Republican nomination for president over Sunrise favorite son, Frank Lowden, who had announced his run for the presidency in Sunrise earlier that year. "Almost" seems to describe not only the presidential hopes but also the life of Sunrise itself. Almost a successful town but relegated to a "could have been" and to a few pages in a history book.

Considered to be the oldest town in Chisago County, Sunrise's first settlers, the Pennsylvania Dutch (German-speaking people) and some Yankees from New England, first came to the area in 1853. Platted in 1856, Sunrise began as a trading post for traders and loggers. Brown's Store was the first building, built in 1853. Blessed with natural beauty, Native Americans were the first in the area and most likely the name of Sunrise was came from those first residents.

A church was organized almost immediately by the Episcopalians in 1853, as an Indian mission church. The

Sunrise, Opera House. (Courtesy of Shawn Hewitt Collection)

Sunrise, 2013. (Author's collection)

300, due in part to the Regional Land Office being located there from 1860 to 1868. In the early days people farmed during the summer and worked the logging camps in the winter.

Sunrise would have its ups and downs, its peaks and valleys. Talk of a railroad coming through the town meant a future. In 1906, it was the Arrow Line, which proposed a route as straight as an arrow from the Twin Cities to Duluth. If so, Sunrise would surely get a station. A track bed grade was started but came to an end just outside of Sunrise. The town would never get a railroad and this surely played into its demise.

Sunrise did have a bank which began in 1916. It was forced to close in 1923 when the cashier was convicted of misappropriation of funds and forging of bank records. He was sentenced to twenty-five years in prison. The bank building later served as a grocery, tavern, and eat shop. Sunrise would be home to many businesses, each with a succession of owners that was hard to keep straight.

At one point Sunrise secured a rowdy and wild reputation. A local dance hall was said to have moonshine and plenty of it. The women were just as plentiful and just as loose and wild. The dance hall later was moved to North Branch and used as an apartment building.

Sunrise went through years of neglect. Buildings fell into disrepair and ruin. Junk and trash lay everywhere. Old businesses moved or closed down. Sunrise had seen better days. In later years, some small businesses would locate in Sunrise, including a pottery shop in the mid-1970s.

Sunrise can boast of another favorite son, Hollywood actor Richard Widmark, who was born in Sunrise in 1914. Though his family moved to Illinois when Widmark was six months old, the actor always considered Sunrise his home town, even visiting the small town during his lifetime. A home-made memorial stands at the site of the Widmark family home.

Most of the old Sunrise is gone but today's Sunrise still has lots of the natural beauty it always had, and several people in the rural area call it home.

church is the earliest in Chisago County records. In 1857, Sunrise was the site of a Native American battle (tongue in cheek), termed the "Cornstalk War." As early history books tell, the battle took place in a field near Sunrise. No real war, it was more of a skirmish or folly. A small group of Native Americans (six to be exact) were zigzagging through stalks of standing corn. In a skirmish, one soldier fell dead as did one native. The other five Native Americans were caught and sent to St. Paul. In court, four of the five were set free with the one considered responsible for the soldier's death held. He was transported to Taylors Falls to await trial. Held at the sheriff's house as no jail was available, the native escaped into the woods of Wisconsin. The whole matter was considered quite a folly.

By the late 1860s, Sunrise had a flour mill, school and several businesses. At its peak, the town had a population of

Dakota County

AUBURN

1856 - 1857

CLASS A

APPROXIMATE LOCATION:
Vermillion Township

Known as a farming village, Auburn was, in reality, more of a railroad platform location for the Hastings and Dakota Railroad than a town. In addition to the platform, a large elevator with a 10,000-bushel capacity was in the town. By 1887, nothing remained of Auburn.

BELLWOOD

1854 - 1860

CLASS A

APPROXIMATE LOCATION:
Junction of Hastings-Cannon Falls-Faribault Road where it was crossed by the Red Wing-Lakeville-Minnesota River Road

Right at the center of the township and smack dab in the middle of fertile farmland, Bellwood was at the junction of the Hastings-Cannon Falls-Faribault Road where it crossed the Red Wing-Lakeville-Minnesota River Road. In the shadow of the Bellwood Catholic Church, the community also had a hotel, the first in the township, which burned twice, and a store. The church cemetery was all that remained in 1975.

CENTRALIA

1856 - 1857

CLASS A

APPROXIMATE LOCATION:
Inver Grove Township

Operating as Centralia for only two years 1856 to 1857, the community was first known as Carlisle 1852 to 1854, and later as Pine Bend 1857 to 1904.

CHRISTIANA

1858 - 1902

CLASS A

APPROXIMATE LOCATION:
Eureka Township

For several years, the small community of Christiana was the only post office in Eureka Township. Due to its location on one of the earliest state mail routes between St. Paul and Faribault, the town thrived for years but was later abandoned.

EAST CASTLE ROCK

1861 - 1897

CLASS A

APPROXIMATE LOCATION:
Castle Rock Township

An early Milwaukee Railroad station town, East Castle Rock was originally called South Hampton. Home to an early post office, which later moved to the southwest corner of the township, South Hampton was renamed East Castle Rock.

ETTER

1871 - 1927

CLASS A

APPROXIMATE LOCATION:
Ravenna Township

A railroad station for the Chicago, Milwaukee, and St. Paul Railroad, Etter also had a post office, a store, and a blacksmith. The tracks were pulled up in 1928-1929 and moved to Prairie Island and the depot building was sold.

Lewiston

1857 - 1871

CLASS A

APPROXIMATE LOCATION:
Sciota Township

Most people couldn't afford to settle in Lewiston. Initially booming in 1857, with a new building going up nearly every week, the town seemed destined for prosperity. Housing a flour mill, blacksmith, hotel, general store, harness and shoe shop, barber, and more, Lewiston offered all the amenities a homesteader could want or need. Also part of the community was a half-mile race track built by founder Charles Lewis. Horse racing was a hobby of his.

But after the initial boom, Lewiston went into decline. Settlers came to the area, but land prices were just too high. People could not afford those prices and moved on to settle in other areas.

The Financial Panic of 1857 was the town's final blow. Heavily mortgaged, the hotel was sold for back taxes and was dismantled. The buyer used the lumber to build a ten-room house and had enough lumber left over to build out buildings. Alvin Houston, area historian, writes that within fifteen years of the first lots being sold, Lewiston was gone. Every building was moved, dismantled or burned except for two, the blacksmith shop, which was moved and converted into a private home and the old school house. The school house was used as the Sciota Town Hall until a new one was constructed in 2006. The school is now being preserved by area residents.

Marshan City
1856
CLASS A
APPROXIMATE LOCATION:

Platted in 1856 and named for land owner Michael Marsh and his wife Ann.

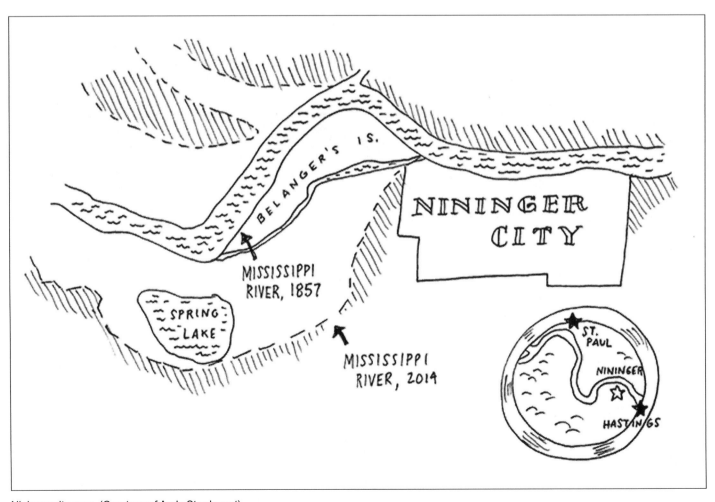

Nininger city map. (Courtesy of Andy Sturdevant)

NICOLS STATION

1867

CLASS A

APPROXIMATE LOCATION:

A flag station on the Omaha Railroad in 1867.

NININGER

1858 - 1860

CLASS A/G

APPROXIMATE LOCATION:
East of Hasting, Minnesota

Ignatius Donnelly was different than most land speculators and town site developers. It wasn't all about the money for him. Certainly financial gain would have been played a role and would have been important, but Donnelly also had loftier goals. Donnelly whole-heartedly believed in Nininger, even spending the rest of his life in the heart of the failed "boom and bust" village.

The area of the proposed town site was first inhabited by Native Americans centuries before the arrival of the Europeans and was known to early settlers as Bluff Landing. The town of Nininger was established in 1856 by Philadelphia and St. Paul real estate businessman, John Nininger. Nininger, who was married to Minnesota Territorial Governor Alexander Ramsey's sister, was himself a large landowner. It can be assumed that being associated with the Ramsey name helped spur promotional efforts as well as lending an air of prestige to the project. Partnering with Nininger was Ignatius Donnelly. The two business partners were well-suited to the shared duties and tasks. Nininger, with his real estate experience, handled the buying and selling of lots, while Donnelly took care of the promotional aspects and the bookkeeping.

In October of 1856 the first lots were sold and bought. There were 3,800 lots, and the asking price was $6.00 each. Riverside lots were sold at upward to $500.00. Several prominent citizens had also invested heavily in the land sales. Sales were brisk and an aggressive nationwide advertising campaign touted the amenities and benefits of the town that included a beautiful view of the river. Easy river access for transportation as well as

Nininger boat landing in recent times. (Courtesy of Andy Sturdevant)

Nininger Town Hall at Little Log House Pioneer Village, Hastings. (Courtesy of the Little Log Pioneer Village)

for water power, good soil for farming and forests full of timber were other attractions. The massive promotional activity spurred sales, and soon the village had 1,000 residents.

A full complement of businesses were located in the burgeoning town and included seven or eight general stores, three or four blacksmiths, wagon shops, a plow factory, a door manufacturer, six saloons, several lawyers and real estate offices, one doctor, one drug store, and three hotels. Future plans called for a public library, Presbyterian church, machine shop, bakery, implement dealer, gunsmith, and tailor among others.

With 100 school-age children in the area, educational needs were met by many private schools. The hoped for public school, however, never materialized. One of the early school meeting places was a pre-emptive shanty with one window. Area historian Leslie Guelcher tells that Native Americans traveling from Pine Bend to Hastings would take a peek in the window to watch the school children at work.

The community also did not have any specified church buildings. Services were conducted in private homes and other facilities.

Nininger location today. (Courtesy of Andy Sturdevant)

Nininger Town sign. (Courtesy of Andy Sturdevant)

Community groups and organizations were very active, and Nininger is considered to have pioneered baseball in Minnesota. The Fourth of July celebration in 1857 was said to have been a grand event.

Though not the founder of Nininger, just a partner, Ignatius Donnelly was a tireless promoter of the town. All records indicate that he thought Nininger his ideal location, as some said, his "Utopia," and he did all he could to support the town, as well as education and culture in the community. Wanting residents to be fully entrenched in the community as a whole, he discouraged out of town speculators. To further settlement by those who would live in the community, he began the Minnesota Emigrant Aid Association. As Dudley S. Brainard wrote in his 1932 history of Nininger, Donnelly offered shares in the association for $25.00 payable in weekly installments. The share offered a ticket from the shareholder's current location to Nininger, a year's provisions and a few farming tools. Since the least expensive ticket from the East Coast was $15.00,

the venture was not a money maker. Donnelly hoped the community eventually would be self-sufficient.

Several factors figured into the demise of Nininger. Chief among them was the inability to secure a railroad through town. Also figuring prominently into the town's demise was the Financial Panic of 1857. Investors were no longer willing to make loans. Banks called in outstanding notes and since Nininger couldn't pay, foreclosure was inevitable. One of Donnelly's residence requirements was that improvements be made upon properties each year. The Panic made that stipulation impossible to meet, and forfeiture was the result. Land values dropped, as did the population, which made recovery for Nininger all the more difficult. Guelcher tells that for some reason, Donnelly lost credibility and investors were even more apprehensive about loaning money. Nearby Hastings was also a factor. With less than half the population of Nininger, Hastings did garner a railroad line and, later, the county seat designation. Though some did stay in the old town site, including Donnelly, Nininger rapidly declined. To his dying days Donnelly stayed loyal to the town, living the remainder of his days in his two-story mansion. He died in 1901. His house, though deteriorating and decrepit, stood until the twenty-first century. Reverting to farmland immediately after the decline of Nininger, the area is now a residential, modern housing development.

PINE BEND

1852 - 1904

CLASS A

APPROXIMATE LOCATION:
Bend of the Mississippi River

Aptly named, Pine Bend was located at a distinct bend in the Mississippi River and surrounded by pine trees. The town was the location of Dakota leader Medicine Bottle's village. The river was key to the establishment of the community in the mid-1850s as river traffic and stage transportation made the town site easily accessible, for a while. Rail transportation soon became the transportation mode of choice and easily replaced earlier methods. When the railroad bypassed Pine Bend, all activity, people, and buildings moved elsewhere. The small village had operated under at least four different names and post office tenures. In the mid 1970s only old cellar depressions marked the location of Pine Bend.

RICH VALLEY

1858 - 1945

CLASS A

APPROXIMATE LOCATION:
Rosemount Township

Lasting nearly seventy-five years, the Rich Valley Post Office was established in 1858 and was discontinued in 1935. The village itself lasted a bit longer. The farming village, with a general store and blacksmith, was named for the area's rich farm soil, Rich Valley was also a station on the Great Western Railroad.

WATERFORD VILLAGE

1854 - 1904

CLASS A

APPROXIMATE LOCATION:
St. Paul to Faribault Road

It took awhile for Waterford to get going. The post office was established in 1854, yet records tell it was 1874 before much business activity got going. In 1874, a general store was built as was a blacksmith shop. In 1878 the Cannon Falls Manufacturing Company opened a mill in Waterford. Located close to Northfield, Waterford could not compete with the larger community and all it offered. In 1975, the town site was a residential community with a community center

WESCOTT STATION

1854 – 1890s

CLASS A

APPROXIMATE LOCATION:
Inver Grove Township

Several rail lines converged at the site of Wescott Station, also known as Radio Center. The town was named for James Westcott, a Civil War veteran who served in the First Minnesota Heavy Artillery.

Hennepin County

Fletcher Hall today. (Courtesy of J. Wagner)

St. Walburga Cemetery today. (Courtesy of J. Wagner)

CHEEVERSTOWN

1847 – 1850s

CLASS A/G

APPROXIMATE LOCATION:
East bank of the Mississippi River, near present day
University of Minnesota

Settled in 1847 on the east bank of the Mississippi River, near the site of the University of Minnesota, the town site was originally platted as St. Anthony City. Locals called it Cheeverstown, after the founder. At the time, there was little settlement on the west side of the river and the east side had a population of over 300. The community included a hotel and for some unknown reason a ninety-foot tower, said to be used for observing the surrounding countryside. Supposedly there was a sign posted that read "Pay your dime and climb."

Thomas Gilsenan writes that a hydraulic ram was installed in the river to furnish water for residents, stage coaches, and travelers. The steam boat *Hindoo*, made regular stops at the town site.

In the 1850s, the City of St. Anthony was established by the Minnesota Territorial Legislature. Encompassing most of the east bank of the river, Cheeverstown was not included within the city boundaries. However, the City of St. Anthony never developed, and Cheeverstown gradually merged with the City of Minneapolis.

EATONVILLE

1829 – 1858

CLASS A/G

APPROXIMATE LOCATION:
Shores of Lake Calhoun

Back in 1829, famed Indian agent (as they were called) Major Lawrence Taliaferro started farming lots on the northeast shore of Lake Calhoun. Farmed primarily for the use of the area's large Native population, a community grew around the farming plots and became known as Eatonville, named for President Andrew Jackson's Secretary of War.

Later the Natives were removed to the south branch of the Minnesota River, and the settlement was abandoned and absorbed into the City of Minneapolis in 1858.

FLETCHER

1900 – 1906 (1960s?)

CLASS A

APPROXIMATE LOCATION:
Junction of Hennepin County 116 and 159 (Territorial Road)

Fletcher developed over a twenty-five-year span. The area's first residents were Bavarian immigrants Andrew and Margaret Stenglein and their family. Settling on an eighty-acre parcel of land in 1855, the Stenglein's later acquired another eighty acres. Their wood-frame home was built at the intersection of Territorial Road (Minneapolis to Monticello) and the Corcoran-Dayton Road. Those two roads quickly became the major transportation routes for the region's residents. Well-maintained with easy access to Minneapolis and other points along the road, travelers could get to wherever they needed or wanted to go using those main arteries.

In 1857 St. Walburga's Catholic Church Parish was organized. A year later a log cabin church was built two miles from the corner junction. Moving to the intersection area in 1883, a new church was constructed as well as a rectory. A cemetery was platted as well. In 1885 a one-room schoolhouse was added to the church complex. Some years later, businesses, houses, and additional buildings began to join the settlement.

By 1895 there was a blacksmith and a meat market/butcher shop. By 1900, four or five other new businesses had joined the growing hamlet. St. Walburga's built a three-story brick-veneer school, with the bricks coming from nearby Dayton.

With an increasing population and a growing business district, residents went to U.S. Congressman Loren Fletcher asking for his help in securing a post office. According to the Hassan Historical Society, the congressman agreed, if the community named the post office after him. Thus, the post office of Fletcher was established in 1901 and was discontinued just five years later, in 1906, with a transfer to Rogers.

The Fletcher Store opened in 1905. The top floor was living quarters for the store owners. The owners also built a house just south of the store to live in during the hot summer. Gas pumps were added in the 1930s. A dance hall/community center was built, which hosted dances, plays, social gatherings, festivals, weddings and other events, in the early 1900s.

Many of the original buildings are still standing, including the three-story brick building at the top of the hill. In 2011 the township of Hassan, of which Fletcher was a part, was officially annexed by the City of Rogers, and Hennepin County became the first in Minnesota without a township.

GREENWOOD CITY

1857 - 1875

CLASS A/G

APPROXIMATE LOCATION:
East bank of the Crow River near Rockford

Hoping to lure people to the Minnesota Territory, the newly established Greenwood Town Site Company launched a widespread and aggressive advertising campaign. Illinois residents by the names of Ames and Florida read the ads with great interest. Having recently moved to Illinois from Maine, the two were looking for new adventures. Married to sisters, the two men headed to Minnesota to start a new town site.

On the Mississippi boat portion of their journey, they met a fellow traveler from Vermont, and soon the three were partners. Arriving at Greenwood City on the Crow River in 1855 they found the site already platted, so they moved down the river towards Rockford. There they met William Frazer, who had already claimed the site. However, Frazer was tired, tired of the work, of the forests and most of all tired of the incessant blood-thirsty mosquitoes. He was only too glad to sell his claim. With winter approaching, settlement plans had to wait until spring. Leaving Ames behind to guard their claim, the other two went back to get their families and recruit settlers.

In 1855, the Minnesota Territorial Legislature passed an act to create a road from Minneapolis to Greenwood. As the crews set out to cut the road, the Greenwood partners and cutting crew met up. The partners helped with the road work and friendships developed. By the time the road reached the Crow River, it had veered north to what is now Rockford. At the time the new settlement had no name. As time went on, Rockford would become the community that survived and still exists today. Greenwood would be relegated to the pages of history.

HARRISBURG

1829 - 1858

CLASS A/G

APPROXIMATE LOCATION:
Brooklyn Center

Harrisburg was one of the few settlements on the West bank of the Mississippi, In 1856 to 1857, a sawmill was built, and 160 acres were platted as Harrisburg.

A hotel, several homes, one or two stores, and a post office were part of the town. A few years later, the sawmill was torn down, one house burned, others were removed, and the land reverted to farmland. In 1873 Harrisburg merged with Brooklyn Center on the Minneapolis to Monticello Road.

HENNEPIN

1850s

CLASS G

APPROXIMATE LOCATION:
Present day Eden Prairie

Now a part of Eden Prairie, Hennepin was a short-lived community on the Minnesota River in today's Eden Prairie. Modeled after town sites in the East, the town began in 1852. Consisting of a sawmill, grist mill, several homes, and a warehouse by the ferry, the village was a major shipping point of grain for several years.

LYNDALE

1892 - 1934

CLASS A

APPROXIMATE LOCATION:
County roads 92 & 6 in Independence

Back in the mid-1800s, a Swedish immigrant put an addition on his log cabin and opened a general store. Once a week, he would haul mail from Maple Plain to the community's small post office, which was then called Hogbo, meaning little town on the hill in Swedish. In 1890, the name was changed to Lyndale.

Reaching its peak before the 1930s, Lyndale included a creamery, a garage, and the Lyndale Lutheran Church. When the railroad came through in 1914, the town moved half a mile. Locals referred to the locations as "Old Lyndale" and "New Lyndale." The new community also included the Lyndale State Bank, a few stores, a lumberyard, feedmill, and blacksmith.

In 1927, the Lyndale State Bank merged with the bank in Maple Plain. The Lyndale Lutheran Church stills stands and is very active. It has been updated and expanded, and the original steeple still stands tall. The original creamery building houses an antique store. The former store and post office is now the Ox Yoke Inn. The garage is also still active. The

Lyndale Church, 1948. (Courtesy of Church member)

Lyndale Church. (Courtesy of Church member)

Dressel's Garage, 2014. (Courtesy of Pastor Gale Reitan)

Former Lyndale Creamery. (Courtesy of Pastor Gale Reitan)

Lyndale 2014. (Courtesy of Pastor Gale Reitan)

Ox Yoke Inn. (Courtesy of Pastor Gale Reitan)

railroad tracks are gone and the old grade is now the Luce Line hiking and biking trail. A highway sign still marks the location. Though no longer a town, the spirit of community lives on in Lyndale.

MINNETONKA MILLS

1920 - 1966

CLASS G

APPROXIMATE LOCATION:
Present day Minnetonka

Witnessing a lot of "firsts" the small lakeside community of Minnetonka Mills had a good start. Home to the first port on Lake Minnetonka, the area's first furniture factory, and the lake's first sawmill, a fire in 1858, which began at the sawmill, destroyed everything. Later, and for a short while, there was a flour mill. Minnetonka absorbed the former town site. Today a Dairy Queen and liquor store are located on the town site.

Former Lyndale school. (Courtesy of Pastor Gale Reitan)

MORNINGSIDE

1920 - 1966

CLASS G

APPROXIMATE LOCATION:
44TH And France Avenue area, Edina

Once the end of the streetcar line in 1900, Morningside was literally across the street from Minneapolis. Area historian Thomas Gilsenan wrote that Morningside voted in 1920 to secede from Edina, which was then a rural community, and become its own entity. With a population at the time of nearly 700, the town had one police officer and contracted with nearby communities, including Edina, for their other municipal services. As Edina developed in to a more urban community, Morningside in 1966, voted to rejoin their former rural community neighbor. Morningside was the first designed residential community in the area, encompassing 8,500 acres, and remains so today. Morningside Hardware is located near the old community and the neighborhood is still referred to as Morningside.

NORTHOME
1882 - 1892
CLASS G
APPROXIMATE LOCATION:
Present day Deephaven

Building his "Nort Home," Charles Gibson of St. Louis began the small community in the late 1800s. A post office operated from 1882 to 1892 (some records indicate 1862 to 1892). According to area historian Thomas Gilsenan, Minnesota's first Frank Lloyd Wright designed home was once located in the community. Gilsenan writes that the home was later torn down and the living room was moved to the Metropolitan Museum of Art in New York. Northome later became Deephaven.

OXBORO

1922 - 1948

CLASS G

APPROXIMATE LOCATION:
11 miles south of Minneapolis, absorbed by Bloomington

Once home to a post office and several businesses, the community name still lives on in a few commercial and area establishments, such as the Oxboro Library and the shopping mall.

Many of the English Oxborough family had settled in the region so it was only natural Thomas would follow his family to Minnesota. Matthew, Thomas's son, grew up in the region and started his farm near the present day Ninety-Fourth and Lyndale intersection. One remnant of the old settlement, George

Sunde's Oxboro Automotive, lasted well into the late twentieth century. Founded in 1927 it was located near Ninety-Eight and Lyndale. As Thomas Gilsanan wrote in his article on Hennepin County towns, the City of Bloomington cleared the area near the town site in the late 1980s as part of a redevelopment project. Today the former town of Oxboro is part of Bloomington.

PERKINSVILLE

1856 - 1861

CLASS A/G

APPROXIMATE LOCATION:
South shore of Lake Independence, just north of Maple Plain

For years I drove pasts the cluster of homes along County Road 19 and the southern boundary of Morris T. Baker Park near Maple Plain, giving little thought as to the history of the area. I now know that these homes, less than a dozen, were located on the town site of Perksinsville.

Platted in 1857 on the south shore of Lake Independence and on the line between Medina and Independence townships, Perkinsville was formed by the Perkins brothers. John and Needham Perkins, who were Quakers, each built a wood-frame house, said to be the first wood-frame houses in the area. A few other homes, as well as a hotel and store were soon part of the town. A brick factory was also built, but it was soon discovered that the area's clay had too much limestone to make bricks and that venture was soon abandoned. The Financial Crisis of 1857 quickly put an end to the brother's plans to achieve municipal status for their settlement. John moved to nearby Maple Plain and became that community's first merchant.

Several homes still occupy the land.

Isanti County

Early Blomford. (Courtesy of Karolyn Lindberg)

Blomford today. (Courtesy of Karolyn Lindberg)

BLOMFORD

1886 - 1904

CLASS A

APPROXIMATE LOCATION:
Near intersection of County Road 5 and County Road 12

Excited about the possibility of shaving two to three hours off his mail route each day, in June of 1909, Blomford's mail carrier began to use a motorcycle to deliver mail, instead of the slower horse and buggy. Things must not have gone as well as planned because an August 1909 news article (just two months later) reported "the mail carrier has lost fifteen pounds using the motorcycle and has returned to using his horse and buggy!"

Blomford, first known as Stormossen or Big Meadow, had a skimming station (part of Spring Vale Creamery), Olson's Blomford Store, a few other stores, and a Partin-Palmer auto

Partin Palmer Ad. (Author's collection)

dealership. The autos sold for around $650.00. The store operated until 1965 when it became the Blomford Clothing Exchange. By 1971, the building was demolished.

BODUM

1899 – 1903 (1950s)

CLASS C

APPROXIMATE LOCATION:
1 mile east of County 19 and 45 (known as Bodum Corner)

Although out of business, the Bodum Store still stands, now a private home. Last summer I had the pleasure of sitting down with the current owners. The historical building had been vacant for some time and restoration was being planned. History was uppermost on the owner's minds, and they had been busy compiling and preserving the history of the store. Their collection includes many binders of photos, from the earliest days to the present, vintage newspaper ads, aerial photos, news articles, and more. To be able to find documentation and then to preserve it forward is a history in the making.

Brush Automobile Ad. (Author's collection)

Bodum store, 1902. (Courtesy of Willard Larson)

FOR SALE AT ALL NEWS STANDS   TEN CENTS A COPY

MOTOR AGE

VOLUME XVIII   CHICAGO, SEPTEMBER 15, 1910   NUMBER 11

Everyman's $485 Car
The Brush Runabout

No matter what your occupation or profession, it will pay you to thoroughly investigate this wonderful car. Find out what it is doing for thousands of merchants, physicians, contractors, engineers, lawyers, salesmen, farmers, mail carriers artisans — in fact, for men (and women) in almost all walks of life.

Write for literature and name of nearest dealer.

BRUSH RUNABOUT COMPANY
811 Massachusetts Ave.,   DETROIT, MICH.
Licensed under Selden Patent

Brush Automobile Ad. (Author's collection)

Bodum's post office lasted only four short years, from 1899 to 1903, but the community outlasted it by decades. A small store at the corner, known as Bodum Corner, later moved a short distance away, near the area's distinctive round barn, still standing. The skimming station began in 1907 and lasted until the 1940s. When it was demolished, the material was used for a

Bodum creamery. (Courtesy of Willard Larson)

garage. Two new stores, one opposite the skimming station opened in 1907. In 1911 an area resident purchased a ten-horsepower Brush automobile for $450.00. He also became the area's auto dealer. His son was a photographer and installed a skylight into the north roof of the store. Today a few buildings still stand, including the Bodum Store, which is now a residence.

DAY

1896 – 1960s

CLASS C

APPROXIMATE LOCATION:
County Roads 22 & 4

Converting the old creamery into a lutefisk processing plant in 1968 worked out great. So great, that forty-six years later, the Day Fish Company is still making the lye-soaked delicacy on a seasonal basis. Now housed in the creamery office, the original plant still stands and is the only business remaining in Day. Open seasonally, from October 1 until the end of January, folks come from far and near to get the lutefisk and other items for sale—walleye, smoked fish from Wisconsin, and other tasty delectables—but it's the lutefisk that is their specialty and draws the crowds. Seasonal workers drop their regular pursuits and work the four-month positions, some had done so for years and decades.

For years, folks in the area have called the town Seven Center because of its location smack dab in the middle of township section seven of Maple Ridge Township. Willard Larson, area historian, writes that there used to be a very old, very large elm tree at the intersection's corner. It was called "Vard Trad" or guardian tree.

Long before the fish company began making lutefisk, Day had a hardware store, tavern, garage, school and store, many of which lasted into the 1960s. A post office operated for twelve years (1896 to 1908) at the turn of the century. Day, as a town, may be gone, but the community spirit is still alive and you can still shop at the historic creamery, but only during the holiday season. It's a great opportunity to see a living piece of history.

Day Fish Company. (Courtesy of WJON Radio)

ELM PARK

1900 - 1902

CLASS A

APPROXIMATE LOCATION:
County road 3 and Holly Street NW

All of Elm Park's buildings are long gone, but Willard Larson, area historian, tells that the front steps of at least one remain in the small park near the old town site.

An early community, Elm Park was established in the early 1900s. Though the post office lasted only two years, the community lasted well into the mid-twentieth century. The store had many owners, and as late as 1949 a garage and auto repair business joined the small business sector. In 1957, the county purchased the land in order to expand County Road 3.

HEWSON

1897 - 1904

CLASS A

APPROXIMATE LOCATION:
Oxford Township

This small community was named for Steven Hewson, a bookbinder at the St. Paul Pioneer Press. The courthouse and jail for the Cambridge District were located at Hewson before Cambridge was designated the county seat.

OLD ISANTI

1865 - 1894

CLASS A/G

APPROXIMATE LOCATION:
Isanti Township, Highway 65

Access to transportation both created and doomed Old Isanti. Because the town of Isanti moved to a spot along the railroad lines and kept the name, the former town site is referred to as "Old Isanti."

The first businesses were located along the Manomin (Ojibwe for wild rice) Trail, which connected Anoka with Brunswick and also Sunrise with Princeton. Needing a source for supplies and overnight lodging, the first two businesses established were a store and a boarding house. Soon others joined the village including a blacksmith, post office (1866 to 1894), a grist mill, a carpenter shop, and a school. A cheese factory had been moved in from Sunrise.

Seemingly situated at an ideal crossroads location, with a steady stream of travelers and a growing population (the school had over 100 students, more than any other district in the county), Old Isanti should have prospered. Cambridge had been the county seat in 1857, when the original Isanti site had been abandoned, so the designation was up for grabs. Both Old Isanti and Cambridge wanted it. The question was resolved when, in 1869, the voters chose Cambridge. Even though Old Isanti was in the southern part of the county, people still traveled the extra miles to do business in Cambridge. Not only could they shop at larger stores, where better variety and lower prices were available, they could also conduct their governmental business in the county seat. Old Isanti simply could not compete with the businesses of Cambridge.

The final blow for Old Isanti was the railroad bypassing the village by little more than one-half mile and going right through Cambridge. The entire village of Old Isanti picked up and moved the half mile to the west and one and one-half miles to the south to be near the railroad. The moved established the Isanti of today while the former town site became known as Old Isanti. Highway 65's four-lanes cover all remains of the old town.

OXLIP

1899 - 1908

CLASS A

APPROXIMATE LOCATION:
Bradford Township

Established in 1886, the Swedish Mission Church of Spencer Brook, later called the Swedish Church of Spencer Brook, had a membership of thirty-nine. Not able to afford much, the first pastor was paid $125 for the first year. The second year his wages increased to $275 a year, with bonuses of five tons of hay, twenty bushels of oats, twenty bushels of corn, and firewood. The ladies of the congregation also spent two days making cheese for the pastor and his family.

Nearly twelve years after the church was established, Oxlip's first store was built with an addition added in 1901. A post office operated from 1899 until 1908.

In 1925 a navy bean sorting system was built. Twelve local women were employed sorting out the bad beans. The venture

Early Oxlip. (Courtesy of Willard Larson)

wasn't profitable and didn't last long. It cost the store more money to sort the beans and package them that they could sell them for.

SPENCER BROOK

1857 – 1940s

CLASS D/G

APPROXIMATE LOCATION:
Just north of County Road 7 and County Road 40 (Spencer Brook Drive)

Realizing the importance of preserving the past for the future, the history-minded folks of past and present Spencer Brook have done just that and more. A sheltered informational kiosk with a detailed map of the long-ago community, plus historical information and photos of the town's businesses and citizens, stands just alongside the present day town hall and the pioneer school building. A special edition booklet, written by Nancy Lavander Seeger with assistance from area residents, family members and area historians and the Isanti County Historical Society tells the story, in words and photos, of Spencer Brook, its people and its businesses. The booklet was used in the creation of the kiosk display.

The Isanti County Historical Society received a grant to restore the old pioneer school building, the county's first school. In kind donations of time, effort, and expenses supplementing the grant, the maintenance and restoration of the historic building are ongoing. For the past few years, the school has hosted a week-long pioneer school, taught by Audrey Misiura (with the help and support of area residents and other history-minded individuals.) One resident gives walking tours of the old town site. Students and teachers dress in period clothing, carry vintage lunch pails and participate in school as it was conducted in the nineteenth century. It is a history they have only read about or seen on television but a truly living history with the present preserving the past for the future.

Long before Europeans arrived, the area was home to the Dakota and the Ojibwe. Father Louis Hennepin was said to have been in the area as early as 1680. The prime location near forested timber land and the easy access of the area's

Spencer Brook Blacksmith. (Courtesy of Isanti County Historical Society and Nancy Lavender Seeger)

Spencer Brook Feed Mill. (Courtesy of Isanti County Historical Society and Nancy Lavender Seeger)

Spencer Brook Grist Mil. (Courtesy of Isanti County Historical Society and Nancy Lavender Seeger)

Spencer Brook United Methodist Church. (Author's Collection)

waterways for transportation and log floating brought the area to the attention of loggers and timber interests. In the 1860s famers came to the area and changed the region to an agricultural base, and, at the same time, changed the lifestyle and economy of the region.

Much of the Spencer Brook history we have comes from the Isanti County Historical Society and the special edition booklet. Spencer Brook began when Benjamin Nichols Spencer established a "hunting camp" on an outlet of Blue Lake. The next year he moved his family to a log cabin near what is now Spencer Brook. Another early family was the Clough family, with fourteen children. One of the children, David, became a Minnesota state senator, lieutenant governor and governor (1887 to 1890). David and one of his brothers later moved to Everett Washington where they established one of the largest lumber mills in the world.

Spencer Brook was home to many of Isanti County's "firsts." The county's first post office was established in 1857. The Spencer Brook school opened in 1858 and was the first school in Isanti County to conduct classes in English. Spencer

Brook Township was one of Isanti County's first townships organized.

The present-day school building was built in 1874 and the first classes were conducted in 1877 for grades one through eight. Regular school terms were held for fall, winter, and spring with, according to the booklet, a special "potato vacation" so students could help with the potato harvest. The booklet also tells that in the sixty-eight-year history of the school, teachers taught over 500 students. Four former students returned as teachers. Closed in 1945, the school district consolidated with the Princeton School District. In 1969 the Spencer Brook Historical Association was formed to restore the old school, and it was then turned over to the Isanti County Historical Society. In 1980, the building was listed on the National Register of Historic Places.

In 1899, the Modern Woodmen of America formed a chapter in Spencer Brook and constructed a hall. The building also served as the Spencer Brook Town Hall and replaced an

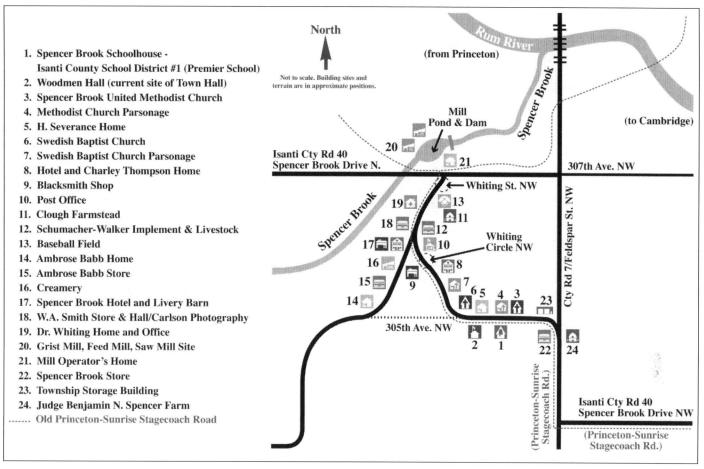

1. Spencer Brook Schoolhouse -
   Isanti County School District #1 (Premier School)
2. Woodmen Hall (current site of Town Hall)
3. Spencer Brook United Methodist Church
4. Methodist Church Parsonage
5. H. Severance Home
6. Swedish Baptist Church
7. Swedish Baptist Church Parsonage
8. Hotel and Charley Thompson Home
9. Blacksmith Shop
10. Post Office
11. Clough Farmstead
12. Schumacher-Walker Implement & Livestock
13. Baseball Field
14. Ambrose Babb Home
15. Ambrose Babb Store
16. Creamery
17. Spencer Brook Hotel and Livery Barn
18. W.A. Smith Store & Hall/Carlson Photography
19. Dr. Whiting Home and Office
20. Grist Mill, Feed Mill, Saw Mill Site
21. Mill Operator's Home
22. Spencer Brook Store
23. Township Storage Building
24. Judge Benjamin N. Spencer Farm
······ Old Princeton-Sunrise Stagecoach Road

Spencer Brook map. (Courtesy of Isanti County Historical Society and Nancy Lavender Seeger)

earlier outdoor platform that was "boarded in" in 1895. When the Woodmen organization dissolved in 1932, the former hall was used primarily as a town hall and community event center. It hosted dances, with the musicians playing on the second floor while the dancers swayed on the first floor. Saturday night movies were also popular in later years.

By the early 1900s the town had, in addition to the school, a Woodmen Hall, two churches with parsonages, a post office, several blacksmiths, two hotels, a creamery, three stores, a photographer, livery, grist mill, feed mill, township storage building, and several homes.

Spencer Brook was home to two churches, the Swedish Baptist Church, which lasted nearly forty years from 1880 until 1920 when services were discontinued and the church dismantled. Many of the furnishings went to the Oxlip Free Church just a few miles down the road. Building the church parsonage put the church group $400 in debt. The pastor's wife wrote John D. Rockefeller asking for money to help pay the debt. No one thought he would answer such a trival request. Shocking everyone, Rockefeller sent $300.00. After

the church's demise, the parsonage was moved to nearby Baxter Lake and was used as a home.

The Spencer Brook United Methodist Church has been going strong since 1898. Originally ministered by itinerant preachers, a permanent clergy arrived in 1896. On land donated by the Clough family in 1898 and with volunteer labor, a church was constructed. Minnesota Governor David Clough, who had grown up in Spencer Brook, gave the dedication. He and his wife donated $300 to help towards the debt. The church was a community center until 1910 when membership declined. After many years of decline a women's group, calling themselves the Sunshine Club, held dinners, auctions, raffles, festivities, sold needlework and eggs, in order to raise funds for restoration of the church. Accomplishing major projects such as a new basement, new steeple, kitchen and fellowship hall, the church has once again become the hub of the community. It is still going strong and still stands on the original plat of land.

A creamery was established in 1897 and that first year produced 900 pounds of butter a week. Though successful, the creamery moved ten miles in 1904, to nearby Crown.

Spencer Brook today. (Author's collection)

Several stores operated under numerous owners throughout Spencer Brook's history. The Spencer Brook Hotel and Livery provided accommodations for traveling salesmen and other travelers. The salesmen would set up their displays in the hotel bar room. Local storekeepers could look over the merchandise available and place their supply orders.

The Smith Store and Hotel was a two-story structure with a warehouse. The top floor hosted dances, meetings and was also a photo studio. Christmas programs were also held there. Traveling medicine shows made stops in Spencer Brook, often staying for a week at a time, putting on different shows each night, complete with the opportunity to purchase bottles of miracle medicine that could cure any and all ailments.

Spencer Brook had its own doctor/dentist. Dr. Whiting was beloved by all. He was appointed the Isanti County physician in 1884. Being a true country doctor, Dr. Whiting made house calls in all weather at all hours of the day or night. He died from pneumonia in 1907 and the Methodist Church could not hold all the people who attended his funeral. Today Whiting Circle and Whiting Street in Spencer Brook are named in his honor.

Spencer Brook's location near the confluence of Spencer Brook and the Rum River allowed several mills to operate including a water-powered grist mill, steam-driven feed mill, and later a sawmill.

As the Spencer Brook Historical Association concludes in its history of the community, advances in transportation and technology changed the economy of the region. By 1920, Spencer Brook was on the decline. Today the history-minded people of Spencer Brook, past and present residents, area historians and the Isanti County Historical Society provide a living legacy of the community. By their efforts, Spencer Brook lives on and its history is preserved for the future.

SPRING VALE

1870 - 1937

CLASS A

APPROXIMATE LOCATION:
Spring Vale Township

After waiting two years for the dam to be constructed, Spring Vale's mill operated day and night. Busy sawing logs during the day, the mill ground grain for cattle feed at night. The dam was destroyed in 1886. No official cause was determined, but speculation was that an unhappy farmer upstream, tired of the continual flooding of his land, may have taken matters into his own hands. Mill owners decided then was as good a time as any to switch the mill over to steam-power.

For a short while a brickyard operated in Spring Vale. Its bricks were yellow rather than the red ones produced in nearby Cambridge. A creamery and Baptist Church were also part of the community. Marilyn McGriff, area historian, writes that Spring Vale never set out to be a trade center; rather businesses were on an as-needed basis. Spring Vale had one of the longest lasting small community post offices in the county, lasting until the late 1930s.

Spencer Brook pioneer school. (Author's collection)

Early Spring Vale. (Author's collection)

Kandiyohi County

Georgeville Creamery. (Courtesy of the Kandiyohi County Historical Society, Willmar)

At Grue Station. (Courtesy of the Kandiyohi County Historical Society, Willmar)

COLUMBIA

1858 - ?

CLASS A

APPROXIMATE LOCATION:
In Spicer – Village Park
Intersection of Lake Avenue and Manitoba Street

By all accounts the 1856/1857 winter was one of Minnesota's severest. *The Kandiyohi County Centennial History* says four feet of light snow blanketed the region, causing widespread hardship. The light, but deep, snow was hard to walk in. Reports say the woods were devoid of wild game, making hunting as a supplemental food source difficult if not impossible. The severe conditions lingered on and prevented the settlers from making supply runs to the nearby river towns until March. When a road from Irving to St. Cloud was opened in the spring of 1857, it was a welcome event. Adding to the excitement was the opening of a tri-county mail route from Henderson to the Columbia area.

Columbia, the town site, was first incorporated in 1857 but that was later dissolved. The town was established in 1858 with a post office until 1862. Briefly in 1861, Columbia was Kandiyohi's county seat. Encompassing 320 acres and platted with broad streets, Columbia had lots of space (whole blocks) reserved for public buildings. Things looked prosperous, at least on paper.

In a 1961 memoir, Elijah Woodcock tells of his family's experiences in Columbia (a nearby lake is named Woodcock). The Woodcocks built Kandiyohi County's first home, located on the Columbia town site. Apparently there was a financial crisis in the Eastern United States with its effects being felt all over the country, especially in the Midwest. In addition, disillusionment with life in the wilderness was setting in. When the railroad line ran through Spicer, Columbia's demise accelerated. Politics became complicated, and through land office neglect, the land on which Columbia was situated reverted to railroad land. With that blow, dreams died, and Columbia faded into history.

FULLERVILLE

1857

CLASS A

APPROXIMATE LOCATION:
North of Willmar on 23/71
East side of frontage road south of County 25

Kandiyohi County's first business firm, the Fuller sawmill, was in Fullerville. Platted in 1857, the town, promoted by Randall Fuller, never materialized. The sawmill and town site were sold and buildings moved to Sauk Rapids in 1861.

GEORGEVILLE

1868 - 1953

CLASS A

APPROXIMATE LOCATION:
4.1 miles East of Belgrade on Highway 55
Right on County Highway 69 for .2 miles

Just three-quarters of a mile from the Kandiyohi-Stearns County line, Georgeville would, over time, call both counties home. Established as a post office in Monongalia County, it would transfer over to Kandiyohi County in 1871 when the two counties merged. In 1888, Georgeville would become part of Stearns County. In the early postal day, residents took turns getting the mail and did so until 1862 when a regular carrier was hired.

An influx of settlers came to the area just as tensions from the Dakota Conflict were peaking. Due to the unrest, a stockade, consisting of four or five log homes, was built in a circle formation. For two months during the winter of 1864/1865, several families, of about twenty-five to thirty people lived in the stockade. Fearing attack at any time, sentinels were posted at night to provide added security.

In the late 1880s, the town had a store, creamery, school, and several residences. For more on Georgeville's later years, *see* Stearns County.

GRUE

1886/1906

CLASS A

APPROXIMATE LOCATION:
Halfway between Willmar and Spicer, a mile East of Eagle Lake

While Grue was an important loading station, that importance was in direct contrast to the community's size. The loading station, named for Ole Nelson Grue, a state senator, was the only building in the community.

HARRISON

1858 - 1907

CLASS A

APPROXIMATE LOCATION:
From Spicer
South on County Road 8 for 3.2 miles
Turn Left on 60th Avenue NE for 5 miles
Turn left on County 4 – near County Park #3

Choosing a spot along the western shore of Diamond Lake, the newly arrived settlers laid out a town and christened it St. John's. To retain the rights to the property, James Campbell lived on the 140 acres over the winter of 1856/1857.

During that time, extensive advertising, especially in the Eastern United States, was conducted, touting Diamond Lake as a very large lake. Settlers poured into the area in the spring and summer of 1857. Disillusioned by the town site, and according to the Kandiyohi Historical Society, deeming the location worthless, the new settlers did however find the lakeside location ideal.

In 1858, James Harris located on the now-abandoned St. John's town site. Along with Amos Dodge, they reorganized and renamed the new town, Harrison. The township would also be called Harrison. It is believed that the first plowing in the county, in 1857, was done in Harrison.

The town did prosper and thrive for a few years. A post office, store, school, churches, and creamery were among the services provided. A cooperative telephone company operated at the turn of the century for a short time, servicing sixty-five phones in the township, twenty-six in Harrison alone.

Farmers in the area were at the whim of the weather and nature. Township records show that at one point, in 1877, the township board voted to assess each male inhabitant five days labor (one day each week for five continuous weeks) for catching grasshoppers.

Many settlers later abandoned their claims. Hard times and the government pre-1863 Homestead Act's stiff time requirements for validating claims proved to be insurmountable, and Harrison became a used-to-be-community.

IRVING

1856 - 1906

CLASS A

APPROXIMATE LOCATION:
East of Spicer MN on County 10
North on County 4 for 2.6 miles

Finding their ideal location on the shores of Cornelian Lake (later Green Lake), the folks from Virginia didn't want to take any chances of losing it. So while the majority of the travelers returned to pull up their stakes and bring their families and belongings to their new-found home, one, Holden Putnam, remained behind. Living in a little shanty through the winter of 1856/1857, Putnam stayed in Minnesota to retain possession of the new town site until the others returned in the spring of 1857.

Laying out the original 160-acre site a two-story, twenty-by-forty-foot hotel was built. In August of that first year, the town acquired an additional 893 acres along the lakeshore and

Harrison store and creamery. (Courtesy of the Kandiyohi County Historical Society, Willmar)

Irving Creamery and Buttertown. (Courtesy of the Kandiyohi County Historical Society, Willmar)

Irving. (Courtesy of the Kandiyohi County Historical Society, Willmar)

which abutted the original 160 acres. Surveyed and platted, everything was readied for the expected "boom" sure to follow and the designation of Irving as the Monongalia county seat, which it was for a brief time.

Area historians report that of all the communities in the county, Irving had more men of means and wealth than any other. Other advantages included the opportune location alongside the new travel route running from Traverse des Sioux to St. Cloud. Many passing through Irving stayed at the newly built hotel.

The Kandiyohi County Centennial History tells that by the time of the Dakota Uprising, only one family, Henry Parsons and his wife, lived in Irving. They resided in the blockhouse, reputedly the largest building in the entire county at the time. That building, as well as the hotel, burned in 1862. The county history also tells that in 1859, gold hunters (forty-two men and three women) on their way to Pike's Peak, camped at Irving and were entertained by the Parsons, even being serenaded by violin and song. However, the boom expected upon Irving's designation as the county seat, never happened. While Irving was making grand plans to become the county seat, their plans were on paper only. Folks in the platted town of Kandiyohi were making plans as well, not only on paper but on the ground. The Kandiyohi boosters set aside a parcel of land said to be the highest elevation in the town. Calling the spot "Capitol Hill," the vantage point afforded a bird's-eye view of not only the town, but the surrounding countryside as well. Such a prominent view would surely appeal to the legislators who could oversee not only all the people but the lake-dotted landscape as well. Acting upon their goals, the Kandiyohi delegation made their influence felt in the legislature.

Realizing that Irving was not ideally located after all nor was it centrally located, the Irving promoters set their sights on a new location, the Southwest shore of Cornelian (later Green) Lake or Fullerville on Eagle Lake, which had already been platted. When all was said and done, that ideal location Holden Putnam held the rights to over the winter of 1856/1857 wasn't so attractive. The town, over its course, would be located in four different spots including near Lake Calhoun and Irving Township, Section 13.

LAKE ELIZABETH

1871 - 1906

CLASS A

APPROXIMATE LOCATION:
East from Willmar on Highway 23E
Right on County Road 4 South
Left (East) on County 86 to Lake Elizabeth Pass and Lane

When the first settlers arrived in the Lake Elizabeth area, Minnesota was a newly designated state. In those early days of statehood, two counties were created in what is now Kandiyohi County. The northern portion was named Monongalia after the early settler's home county in Virginia and the southern county was called Kandiyohi. Twelve years later, in 1870, voters agreed to legislation merging the two counties into one, to be called Kandiyohi.

After the first setters came to Lake Elizabeth, tensions between the Native Americans and immigrant settlers escalated, and it wasn't long before full-scale war broke out. Fearing for their well-being and seeking safety in numbers, the entire population left the region, all on the same day! Taking all the belongings they could, even their cattle or at the least turning them loose, the settlers fled to Clearwater and on to Anoka. Hoping to return to gather the rest of their personal belongings, the settlers asked Governor Ramsey for assistance. According to a Kandiyohi County history, Governor Ramsey supplied five muskets and ordered an escort. For the sake of safety for both settlers and escorts, the military disregarded the governor's order, saying it would take three hundred soldiers to ensure safety and with only one hundred on hand, there were not enough to undertake the journey. Not to be deterred, the settlers hired a team and made the journey with four brave Norwegians as escorts.

After the danger was over, all but one of the settlers, returned to Lake Elizabeth. Once arriving, the second settlement of Lake Elizabeth experienced a spurt of strong growth. A post office was established, with the name Lake Elizabeth coming from the wife of a prominent lawyer in Forest City. The post office would serve a large area. Soon the community would have a creamery, store, twenty-three homesteads, and a nearby school. First holding classes in different homes, the granary, and even outside when the

Lake Elizabeth creamery, 1904. (Courtesy of the Kandiyohi County Historical Society, Willmar)

Lake Elizabeth, 1904. (Courtesy of the Kandiyohi County Historical Society, Willmar)

temperatures were oppressive, a log school was eventually built. At the annual Christmas program in 1874, the school's ceiling caught fire due to an old stovepipe and the building partially burned. It was repaired and used until 1885 when a new, larger school was constructed.

The town continued for many years. The store added gas pumps in 1915 and a hatchery in 1922. In 1921 the creamery pioneered the Land O'Lakes Association. However, in 1928 the creamery was sold to a private interest, and it closed in 1936. The next year, 1937, would see the demise of the town of Lake Elizabeth. Many buildings were moved to the new village of Lake Lillian as well as being repurposed as private dwellings.

NORWAY LAKE (JERICHO)

1867 - 1914

CLASS A

APPROXIMATE LOCATION:
Marker is located at County Road 40 on County Road 10
(one mile)

Lasting several years, the settlement of Norway Lake, also known as Jericho, was established in 1879. Soon the town consisted of two general stores, the Norway Lake Lutheran Church, a creamery, feed mill, blacksmith, wagon shop, shoe store, and several residences. A few homes and a store were all that remained in the 1970s.

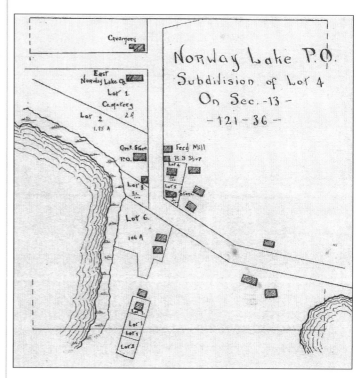

Norway Lake (Jericho) layout. (Courtesy of the Kandiyohi County Historical Society, Willmar)

Norway Lake (Jericho) street scene. (Courtesy of the Kandiyohi County Historical Society, Willmar)

Norway Lake (Jericho) creamery. (Courtesy of the Kandiyohi County Historical Society, Willmar)

PRIAM

1900 - 1908

CLASS A

APPROXIMATE LOCATION:
South on Minnesota 23 for 18.3 miles

No longer existing as a town, Priam was a station on the Willmar and Sioux Falls Railway. The town consisted of an elevator, school, creamery, and a few homes. In 1903, the creamery was converted to a church, which no longer exists. Priam was also home to a well-known 4-H group, the Priam Pilots. The school also served as a community center and hosted several events and get-togethers. Plays were especially popular.

WHITEFIELD

1856-1857

CLASS A

APPROXIMATE LOCATION:
South of Willmar on U.S. 71 .1 mile on 60th Avenue SE

Working his way across the United States, English-born Edwin Whitefield, made his living by selling prints of his watercolor paintings of the towns he visited. Whitefield arrived in Minnesota in 1855 and settled into Kandiyohi County the next year. Whitefield would be the first to come upon Lake Lillian, which he named for his wife. That same year, 1856, Whitefield, along with a group of investors formed the Whitefield Exploring Company. In addition to Whitefield, the group also platted the Kandiyohi town site and hoped for the state capitol to be located there. As for the town of Whitefield, it was established in 1856, incorporated in May of 1857 and was later vacated.

Lac Qui Parle County

Lac Qui Parle Town site. (Courtesy of A. Filer)

Lac Qui Parle Town Hall today. (Courtesy of A. Filer)

HAYDENVILLE

1878 - 1930s

CLASS A

APPROXIMATE LOCATION:
6 Miles West of Madison on County 40

Things sometimes got a little wild in Haydenville. In 1929 the elevator burned to the ground. Sam Olson of the Lac qui Parle Historical Society writes that the damages were $18,000 and the loss of 10,000 bushels of grain. Two years later the roof of the Haydenville Dance Pavilion blew off and landed alongside a neighboring store. That same year two armed men walked into the store, demanded that the cash register and safe be opened. They then handcuffed the owner and left with cash, stealing oil and gas on their way out.

Established in 1878, but not platted until 1901, by Herbert Hayden, the small railroad, farming community was located on the Minneapolis and St. Louis Railroad. The town was home to several businesses including a bank (which later moved to Madison, Minnesota), a general store, lumberyard, grain elevator, and school.

After Haydenville's decline, the land reverted to farmland.

LAC QUI PARLE VILLAGE

1870 - 1907

CLASS A

APPROXIMATE LOCATION:
Southwest of Lac Qui Parle State Park, near County 20 and Rochester Avenue

On the surface, county seat designation doesn't seem all that important. Yet history has proven that it can make or break a town's very existence, as it did in several Minnesota counties. Thus, competition was tough, contentious, heated and could be downright nasty and outrageous at times. Often rival communities would steal county and courthouse records, but Lac Qui Parle County has that beat. They kidnapped the entire courthouse.

When Lac qui Parle was formed in 1887, the county seat was in the Village of Lac Qui Parle, for which a wood-frame courthouse had been built. The multi-purpose building also housed the court and county offices, a post office, and a hotel.

The Village of Lac Qui Parle was an early settlement in the region. There had been two other town sites in the township, Williamsburg and one other, which was unnamed. Both communities had stores which were moved to Lac Qui Parle Village in the late 1860s. Long before there was a town, the site had been home to Native Americans. A nearby mission, the Lac Qui Parle Mission was founded in 1835 and is now a Minnesota Historical Society site.

In 1871, the village established postal services. The first mail was carried by a messenger hired by the settlers. The *Lac Qui Parle County Press* was published from 1872 to 1878. Another newspaper, the *Lac Qui Parle Independent* also began that year.

In 1898, a battle between Madison and Dawson was waged for the county seat designation. Hoping to gain the upper hand in the contest, 150 men and forty wagon teams rode into Lac Qui Parle Village and quite literally took the courthouse. Battling broken axles and an early snow storm, they hauled the building and placed it on the present day court house site. Ten years later a new court house was built. Original oak wood can be found in that courthouse to this day, in the counter tops, cabinets, stairs, doors, and more.

Lac qui Parle never secured rail service and with the loss of the county seat, faded into history.

Lac Qui Parle Village today. (Courtesy of A. Filer)

McCleod County

Acoma

1892 - 1905

CLASS A

APPROXIMATE LOCATION:
Acoma Township

Founded in 1857, a post office operated from 1892 to 1905. At its peak the town had twelve buildings, which included a church, school, creamery, ice house, blacksmith, feed mill, and dance hall.

Bear Creek

1870s

CLASS A

APPROXIMATE LOCATION:
4 Miles south of Silver Lake, Rich Valley Township

One of the first things the Czech Catholic settlers did was build a church. Constructed in 1872, the Bear Creek Church merged with St. Joseph's Church in Silver Lake and the Bear Creek location was considered a mission church of St. Joseph's. Eventually the Bear Creek church was closed with only the cemetery remaining. The McLeod County Historical Society writes that in the early days, the region was frequented by bears, thus the name, Bear Creek.

Bear Lake

1899 - 1903

CLASS A

APPROXIMATE LOCATION:
NE of Hutchinson

Established over 100 years ago, the Bear Lake Ladies Group, known as the Bear Lake Sunshine Society, was still going strong in 2010. The former community had a store, creamery, hall, and school.

Brush Prairie

1867 - 1883

CLASS A

APPROXIMATE LOCATION:
3 Miles south of Lester Prairie

Built in 1859 in the community of Brush Prairie, the Bergen Norsk Evangelical Lutheran Church was at the center of the community. In 1875 a parsonage was added. When the church burned in 1896, a new church was built.

Cedar City

1859 - 1863

CLASS A

APPROXIMATE LOCATION:
Lynn Township

One of Cedar City's first settlers was Daniel Cross. His daughter Mary is considered to be the first white child born in McLeod County. Cross built a cabin in Cedar City in 1857 but moved to Meeker County in 1859. Cross was killed by Native Americans on September 23, 1862.

Clear Lake

1912 - 1963

CLASS A

APPROXIMATE LOCATION:
On shores of Clear Lake

Always at the heart of the community, the Clear Lake store was built in 1912 and operated until 1983. An early resident recalls that, when television came out, area residents went to the store to view the new contraption, especially on Saturday mornings when the wrestling shows were televised.

COLLINS

1871 - 1879

CLASS A

APPROXIMATE LOCATION:
10 Miles South of Hutchinson (Stewart)

In Collins, life centered on the Collins store. On Sunday afternoons, ball games, trapshooting, and horse shoes were common activities. In the early days, supplies were brought in by team and wagon, later by automobile.

The community's first school was a white one-room building. A two-story brick school was constructed in 1921 and included a library, indoor toilets, and a basement with kitchen and dining facilities. One hot-food item a day was made to go with the sandwhiches brought from home. The store closed in the 1950s. A private home is located on the site.

A post office operated from 1871 to 1879 and was first called Collins Post Office but was later renamed Stewart Post Office. The Chicago, Milwaukee, and St. Paul Railroad had a station called Collins and also one called Stewart, each in different township sections. Stewart, the city, later separated from the township.

FERNANDO

1899 – 1903 (1970s)

CLASS A

APPROXIMATE LOCATION:
6 Miles south of Stewart

Fernando's Round Grove Can Creamery was said to be the last local creamery in Minnesota to close. Named for the buttermaker, Ferdinand Fenske, the community was born out of the need for a church. Needing a place to worship, the German settlers built one in 1890 and a parsonage two years later. Eight years after the construction of the church, the creamery started operations. A general store was built in 1901 and closed in 1975 and is now a private home. The post office was short-lived operating from 1899 to 1903.

When the garage/auto dealershop closed in 1931, after seven years of existence, the building was converted to a tavern, which closed in 1944. St. Matthew's Church and a few buildings remained at the town site into the late twentieth century/early twenty-first century.

FREMONT

1856 - 1867

CLASS A/G

APPROXIMATE LOCATION:
North shore of Silver Lake

Surprisingly and most confusing, the post office of Fremont was established in Hennepin County in 1856 and was transferred to McLeod County in 1859. To further complicate the history, a farm post office was established in 1867 as Silver Lake but was called Fremont until the general store was built and the town site was laid out as Silver Lake. Supposedly, Fremont had a store and a few houses.

KARNS CITY

1857

CLASS A

APPROXIMATE LOCATION:

The "L" shaped town site included a hotel, which was a two-story all brick building. It had a roof, but no windows. The town was abandoned during the Panic of 1857. The log hotel was burned to the ground during the Dakota Uprising of 1862.

KOMENSKY

1899 - 1903

CLASS A

APPROXIMATE LOCATION:
Hutchinson Township

Community involvement was important to the early Czech settlers in Komensky. One of the very first things they did was organize the Bohemian Reading and Educational Society. Dues were ten cents a month and the society purchased Czech books, established a Czech choir (with over fifty members) and built the Bohemian Hall. The hall was a local landmark and institution. The hall hosted meetings, school events, weddings, showers, anniversaries, and dances. Operating until the 1940s it was torn down in the 1960s and the lumber was used to build a house.

Komensky also had the Luce Line Railroad, a store, elevator, creamery, stockyard, ice house, several homes, and a beet dump/scale house, which was used to weigh sugar beets grown for the Sugar Beet Corporation of Chaska.

As transportation modes changed, the rail line in Komensky closed. Business slowed. Komensky's buildings were moved or torn down. Only the school remained.

KONISKA

1860 - 1882

CLASS A

APPROXIMATE LOCATION:
6 Miles north of Glencoe on South fork of Crow River

Women were a rare sight in early Koniska and their absence played a role in the naming of the community, or so the story goes. According to the McLeod County Historical Society, four single men settled claims near the site of Koniska, each building their home at the corner of their claim. A Native American chief visited one of the homes and asked where the women were. When told there were none, he exclaimed "Koniska," meaning bachelor home and the name stuck.

It seems that the absence of women was a hindrance to the growth of the community. With a population of fifty-three and only one being female, the area newspaper extolled the need for women to join the community. The McLeod County Historical Society tells of an article in the *Henderson Democrat*. The article states that women were sorely needed and would go "like hotcakes." It was also noted that the women would find no better men than those in Koniska. The men, it continued, were willing to have wives; they just didn't have the time to go East to hunt for them.

The Glencoe Coop Creamery established a skimming station at Koniska, and area farmers would take turns delivering the milk to Glencoe.

Money was appropriated for the construction of a bridge across the river but it took ten years before the bridge was a reality. Rowboats were used to carry passengers and goods across the river until the bridge was completed. In 1973, the McLeod County Commissioners put the bridge up for sale. The McLeod County Historical Society writes that only one bid, for $500, was received. It was decided to designate the bridge a historical site. Bypassed by two railroads, one going to the north, the other to the south, Koniska would fade into history. The bridge and a cemetery are all that remains.

LAKE ADDIE

1856

CLASS A

APPROXIMATE LOCATION:
Now Brownton

Going through several name changes, the town was first known as Grimshaw's settlement. The name Lake Addie, supposedly came from a young woman from Minneapolis who visited the Grimshaws in 1856. Later the Brown family settled in the area. Two of the Brown brothers went off to fight in the Civil War and only one returned. When a rail station was established away from Lake Addie, the growing area near the rail line was platted by Alonzo Brown, the one Civil War soldier returning, as a town site. In memory of his fallen brother he named it Brownton. Lake Addie was platted as well and is a subdivision of Brownton.

ROCKY RUN

1860 - 1874

CLASS A

APPROXIMATE LOCATION:
6 Miles west of Winsted

McLeod County's first church was St. John's the Baptist Church built by the French Canadian settlers of Rocky Run. Primarily a stopping point on the way from Hutchinson to Minneapolis, the church and a rural community were the only settlements in the area. The church later burned to the ground due to a lightning strike. The post office for Rocky Run, in 1870, transferred to Carver County.

SHERMAN STATION

1917 - 1950s

CLASS A

APPROXIMATE LOCATION:
Halfway between Winsted and Silver Lake

Sherman Station's dance hall was considered the place to go for a good time in the 1930s, 1940s and 1950s. Many a wedding dance was held in the hall as were other events. Free movies were also shown.

Established in 1917 as a station on the Luce Line, Sherman Station was a four-block town with a store (moved in from Pleasant Hill) and a few station buildings. The Luce Line Raildroad, records say, was one of the most reliable. The winter of 1917 was especially brutal with heavy snows and blowing winds that caused deep snow drifts. Even so, while other railroads experienced numerous delays and stalls, the Luce Line had only one.

As dependence on the railroad dwindled, so did Sherman Station.

SOUTH SILVER LAKE

1881 - 1890s

CLASS A/G

APPROXIMATE LOCATION:
4 Miles south of Silver Lake, Rich Valley Township

Building a line through the area in 1886, the St. Paul, Minneapolis, and Manitoba Railway, routed three miles south of Silver Lake, through the 1881 platted town of South Silver Lake. A bustling community grew around the depot and included a livestock shipping yard, saloon, two general stores, a millinery shop and a livery. Providing easy access to the town and points along the rail line, a passenger train left South Silver Lake for Minneapolis at 7:30 A.M. and returned each evening at 7:30 P.M. It is said that many traveling salesmen and businessmen took advantage of the scheduled routes. All of the area's mail was routed through South Silver Lake. When the Luce Line established a station to the north of Silver Lake, it was only a matter of time before South Silver Lake ceased to be. Eventually the businesses and residents moved to the new railroad town. There were few remains in 1989.

ST. GEORGE

1870 - 1880

CLASS A

APPROXIMATE LOCATION:
6 Miles north of Glencoe on South fork of Crow River

Utilizing the Crow River's water power, an early dam was built that powered the town's grist and saw mills. Other businesses in the five-acre town site were a general store, blacksmith, shoe shop, creamery, church, a few homes and three saloons. The town came to an end with the railroad's bypassing of the community. Nothing remains of the town but several families live in the area.

WEST LYNN

1883 - 1900s

CLASS A

APPROXIMATE LOCATION:
McLeod County

Prior to the church being built in 1883, the German settlers had held services in their homes. The community formed around the church and included a general store and a creamery. The store, operated by a succession of owners, the last being the Homberg family. The store closed when Wally Homberg entered the service during World War II and was killed in the Battle of the Bulge. Opened in 1901, the creamery closed in 1989. All the buildings were sold.

WEST WINSTED

Early 1900s - 1960s

CLASS A

APPROXIMATE LOCATION:
6 Miles west of Winsted

Though the community included a creamery and an ice house, the tavern was the main attraction. The McLeod County Historical Society writes that the tavern had two nickel slot machines, which at the time were illegal. One resident recalled that when word came that the "feds" were on their way, the slot machines were loaded into a wagon, taken to a nearby home and hidden under blankets until the threat was gone.

The McLeod County Historical Society also writes that in 1938 Highway 7 was built and the tavern was too close to the road, so it had to be moved. The owners, instead, tore the tavern down and built a new, larger one. Later the tavern was moved to Lester Prairie and a restaurant was added. Another added attraction was the live bears on display. Sold in 1960, it remained a bar until 1965.

Meeker County

Second Acton Creamery (Hope Lake Creamery). (Meeker County Historical Society)

First Acton Creamery

Hope Lake Creamery was destroyed by a fire Aug. 2, 1919. The contents, ice house, coal shed, and boiler were destroyed. It was 18 years old. It was insured for $3,000. The stockholders met and decided to rebuild. Milk was hauled to Litchfield, Rosendale, and Star Lake.

First Acton Creamery (Hope Lake Creamery). (Courtesy of the Meeker County Historical Society)

ACTON

1857 – 1904 (1940s)

CLASS C

APPROXIMATE LOCATION:
County Road #23 between County #1 and County #4

When Meeker County historian Gerry Moen offered to give me a driving tour of Meeker County's lost towns, I jumped at the chance. Picking me up on a later September morning, Gerry had our route planned. More organized than I could ever hope to be, she had a map marked out, folders containing photos and historical information on each location we were going to visit and a plan of action. She had even done some scouting of the locations.

Our first stop was a short distance from Litchfield. Driving along County Road #23, which I later learned is called the Acton Road as it stretches from County Road #1 to County Road #4. Acton will forever be linked with the beginning of the Dakota Conflict as the first casualties of the uprising occurred near Acton. The "Acton Incident," in summary, involved four young Dakota men returning from hunting and seeing some eggs in a nest on the farm of a white settler. An argument developed as to whether or not, the four should take the eggs. One of the young men refused to take the eggs, and another dared him to prove he wasn't afraid of the white man. Attempting to prove his bravery, they met up with the settler and a shooting match ensued. After the contest was over, the Dakota reloaded and killed the settler and four others. Returning to their village, they told their story to the chiefs who, knowing the gravity of the situation, knew war was at hand. Thus began the Dakota Conflict.

Acton store today. (Author's collection)

Second Acton Creamery (Hope Lake Creamery). (Courtesy of the Meeker County Historical Society)

89

Acton remnants. (Author's collection)

Acton store scenes. (Mary Koch/Gerry Moen)

Acton was just a log parsonage in the early 1860s and didn't develop into a community until the late 1860s. Acton was located along the Henderson-Pembina Trail by Hope and Long Lakes. The first store opened in 1867, switched owners many times until the store's closure in the 1930s. A co-op creamery was established in 1899 with a ninety-nine-year lease on the land. Called the Hope Lake Creamery, the first building was a wood-frame structure that burned in 1920. It was replaced with a brick-and-tile building. Butter was churned until the late 1920s when the co-op disbanded and the business was taken over by a private owner who continued operating the creamery and making butter until 1942 when it was sold again. Used as a warehouse and truck garage, the

Acton site today. (Author's collection)

Acton store today. (Author's collection)

building, in the 1950s was converted to raising turkeys. The building was torn down in the 1970s.

The Acton Telephone Company began operating in the early 1900s and discontinued in the 1940s. The switchboard operators first boarded in the store and later in the building just to the west of the store.

As Gerry pulled to the side of the road, I didn't immediately see much of anything. Then I saw it, there in the shadows of the large trees and overgrown brush I saw the shape of an old building. There stood the old store building and alongside of it, the telephone company building. Obscured by brush and foliage the buildings were nearly indiscernible to the auto traffic speeding by. Much like the history of the old town, discovering the history is akin to uncovering the hidden past.

Collinwood, 1868. (Courtesy of the Meeker County Historical Society)

blacksmith, hotel, post office, dance hall, and saloon were active businesses, although the dance hall, called the Klondike was short-lived and was destroyed by fire. The railroad was slated to go through the community but one land owner refused to sell his land, so the route was changed one mile north causing Collinwood its fatal blow. Little remains of the community today.

COLLINWOOD

1869 - 1878

CLASS A

APPROXIMATE LOCATION:
Collinwood Township

Called Little Virginia in 1866, the community's name changed to Collinwood in 1870. A grist mill was located on the north shore of Lake Collinwood. A

CORVUSO

1898 - 1953

CLASS E

APPROXIMATE LOCATION:
Meeker County Road #7 and County Road #1

Originally located one mile east and one and one-half miles north of its present location, Corvuso, meaning gathering place for crows in corrupted Latin, was

Corvuso, 2014. (Courtesy of Gerry Moen)

Corvuso Meats. (Courtesy of Gerry Moen)

primarily a farming community and still is. In 1860 the land was purchased by the General Land Office of the University of Minnesota, in 1887, a St. Paul judge bought the land and shortly thereafter the town of Corvuso developed. Early businesses included an elevator in 1922, which was torn down and rebuilt in Silver Lake in 1934; a hardware/lumberyard, which later burned; a beet dump; general store; and tavern. The tavern lasted until 1979 and is now a private home. The post office closed in 1953, the creamery in 1982. Corvuso is today known for the meat processing plant which residents say has the best sausage.

Corvuso today. (Courtesy of Gerry Moen)

CROW RIVER

1867 – 1909 (1940s)

CLASS A

APPROXIMATE LOCATION:
1 mile South of County 3 and 520th Avenue

Crow River store, early 1900s. (Courtesy of the Meeker County Historical Society)

Crow River site, 2014. (Gerry Moen)

Nearly every community in the late 1800s had a creamery. Without refrigeration, nearby facilities for milk were necessary. Area farmers brought in their milk in ten-gallon cans, three times a week, to be separated. The can was washed, steamed and returned to the farmer. Each farmer had a number for record keeping. If a farmer wanted to take some skim milk home for feeding livestock, they would use a different can. The milk was then made into butter and sold. A general store was generally located near the creamery and the two businesses were the hub of the community.

In 1916, the Crow River Creamery building burned and it was replaced with a cement block building. The *Meeker County Memories* book tells how the cement blocks were made. Area resident Frank Marshall devised a frame with a lever. The moist cement was poured into the frame, allowed to dry and set. The lever was then released which pushed the block out so another could be made.

The Crow River post office was short-lived. The store lasted sixty-three years from 1912 until 1964. In 1912, the store's gas pump pumped one gallon at a time. After a newer, larger pump was installed, the old pump was used for kerosene.

The Creamery Store, Crow River, 1909. (Courtesy of the Meeker County Historical Society)

Crow River store was across from the church, 2014. (Gerry Moen)

Crow River creamery site, 2014. (Gerry Moen)

Scene at Crow River. (Courtesy of the Meeker County Historical Society)

In 1964, an auction was held at the store, everything from store goods to antiques, the building, and the property were sold. The buyer later tore the store building down. Little else remains of the town.

EAST KINGSTON

1860s – 1930s

CLASS B

APPROXIMATE LOCATION:
Northeast of Kingston (Off 318th Street near Hwy. 15)
near Lake Francis

Kingston was a popular location name in the area. There is the present day small town of Kingston. Then there are the used-to-be towns of North Kingston, East Kingston and, as long-time resident Marlyn Anderson tells me, there was also a West Kingston, but that never developed into much. So many Kingstons proved to be a bit confusing.

Marlyn and his father were both born in East Kingston. His grandfather had settled in the area in the 1890s. The small community was located on Eagle Creek that runs out of nearby Lake Francis. The lake was rather shallow and very nearly went dry in the 1930s and froze out during the winter, killing all the fish. Marlyn remembers his father talking about a large resort on the nearby lake at one time it had twenty-one cabins.

In 1866, Jefferson Carville and Dr. A.H. Carville erected a dam in what would become East Kington. The following year the Carville brothers built a grist and saw mill on the site. East Kingston was platted in 1871 by Jefferson Carville upon the northeast quarter of Section 14 and the plat filed for record on January 24, 1871. The Carville brothers operated the mill from 1867 to 1873 when Dr. Carville sold his share to John Norgren. The mill operated under the name of Carville & Norgren until about 1885 when it went into litigation.

Remains of the East Kingston dam. (Courtesy of Barb Richardson/Robyn Richardson)

EAST KINGSTON 1980

Carvill Mill
Eagle Creek & Dam
Main Street
Stone Bridge

Stone bridge over Eagle Creek, Main Street. (Courtesy of Barb Richardson/Robyn Richardson)

A stone bridge and an earthen dam were built on the creek and provided power for a sawmill and a flour mill. Maryln told me that some residents would carry fifty-pound sacks of wheat over eight miles to go the mill to get it ground. The mills and East Kingston were short-lived, lasting only about ten years. A small store and feed store were also part of the town.

East Kingston declined as did the other Kingstons in the area. Maryln recalled that the present town of Kingston, used to be a booming town. It had three or four gas stations, three bars, a grocery, and more.

In later years, Robyn Richardson's parents owned the former town site property. Robyn's father was a skilled stone mason, and he repaired and restored the stone bridge over the creek. Robyn's mother, Barb Richardson, was so interested in East Kingston's history she researched the site and located some of its history and original plat of the town at the Litchfield Public Library.

Left: East Kingston bridge; Right: Mill Stream Bridge. (Courtesy of Barb Richardson/Robyn Richardson)

Barb also documented the town in photos and words. She wrote a memorial titled "The Ballad of East Kingston" and it is a fitting tribute to many lost towns. The lyrics in part are:

"Born a Frontier Town,
Promises Did Abound
"The Coming Railroad
Will Prosper the Town.

Mercantile Store
New Blacksmith Shop Did Stand
The Village Smithie
Hammer in Hand

Oh, Sad East Kingston Town
Where is Your Promise Now?
No Railroad Did Appear
So Townsfolk Disappeared
Leaving Behind a Ghost Town.

FOREST CITY

1857 - 1907 (1960s)

CLASS E/F

APPROXIMATE LOCATION:
County Road #24 6 miles north of Litchfield

Forest City has a long historic heritage with a legacy of Meeker County "firsts." Designated the Meeker county seat from 1857 until 1869, the firsts include: the first

Welcome to Forest City. (Author's collection)

97

Early Forest City Creamery. (Courtesy of the Meeker County Historical Society)

Forest City Creamery today. (Author's collection)

Forest City Store today. (Author's collection)

store (Atkinson) in 1856, the first post office (1856), first Masonic Lodge (1867), first school (1857), first newspaper (*The News*, 1868). The first white girl born in Meeker County was born in a covered wagon while her family was camped at Forest City while enroute to Harvey Town.

The community grew rapidly. A steam-powered sawmill was operating by 1858. By 1865 a flour mill was also operating. A brickyard was established in 1858. A creamery operated until 1929. The first creamery building was wood-frame and was replaced by the present standing building in 1929.

In 1868, Meeker County's first newspaper, called *The News*, was printed on a printing press said to be the first ever brought to Minnesota. The flour mill operated nearly fifty years from 1865 until 1914 when the dam washed out and the mill was dismantled.

Gerry Moen, considers Forest City her hometown. She vividly recalls going to Forest City in the 1930s and 1940s, with her parents. Her dad went to Forest City to grind corn and grain at the feed mill. He also had repair work done in town. Her mother, took eggs to the store. On Saturdays, the area children would sit on blankets outside the store and watch movies. Her parents bought the kids ice cream cones for five cents. During the summer time an occasional traveling carnival came to Forest City. Rides were a treat, and Gerry recalls that a photographer would take photos of people and

then offer to sell them a photo. For years, Forest City had a large iron bridge over the Crow River. Some residents recall a Halloween prank of climbing the bridge and dropping eggs on the passing cars.

When Litchfield was designated the county seat in 1869, and with the arrival of the railroad in Litchfield as well, Forest City declined. Today the creamery still stands as do other buildings, such as a school (the third school building), two active churches, a tavern, and several homes. A weathered welcome sign tells a brief history of Forest City and the Dakota Conflict. There are two parks in the area—one displays a historical marker in memory of those lost during the Conflict. Though most of the businesses are closed and gone, the town site still has a community feel. Just south of Forest City stands the Forest City Stockade and a recreation of 1862 Forest City.

There is mention in more than one resource of a phenomenon called the "Indian Ghost Hill." Cheryl Bulau wrote that the phenomenon defies gravity. On a hill not far from Forest City, a gravity anomaly or magnetic vortex or spirits cause a car to be pulled up the hill. She quotes Terry Shaw directions which are: Take County Road 2 north out of Forest City. Go 1.5 miles from the bridge to 330th Street, turn right and go half a mile to 660th Street, turn right again and drive up the small hill. The hill is just before the curve to the left. Turn around to face north and take note that it is downhill in front

Forest City School today. (Author's collection)

Forest City. (Courtesy of the Meeker County Historical Society)

of and behind you. Drive about half way down the hill and stop. Place your car in neutral and take your foot off the brake. It seems you are being pulled back up the hill. Some say it is the spirits of Natives pulling you away from their sacred hunting grounds. Could it be?

FOREST CITY STOCKADE

1976 - PRESENT

CLASS H

APPROXIMATE LOCATION:
County Road #24 6 miles north of Litchfield

You can't get any closer to experiencing life in a long ago lost town than you can at the Forest City Stockade near Litchfield. On an unseasonably warm late September afternoon, I walked the streets of 1862 Forest City. On a personal tour with Bob Hermann, one of the board members of the stockade, we stopped to browse the general store, checked the post office for mail, visited the chapel and toured several other buildings. Serenely quiet, the history is palpable and a sense of reverence is permeating. No, I didn't travel by time machine to the past. Thanks to a group of dedicated, hard-working volunteers, the Forest City Stockade is a homage and memorial to the early pioneer settlers of the area and you too can visit the site.

Begun as a restoration project in American's Bicentennial year (1976), the stockade, stands near its original location, is

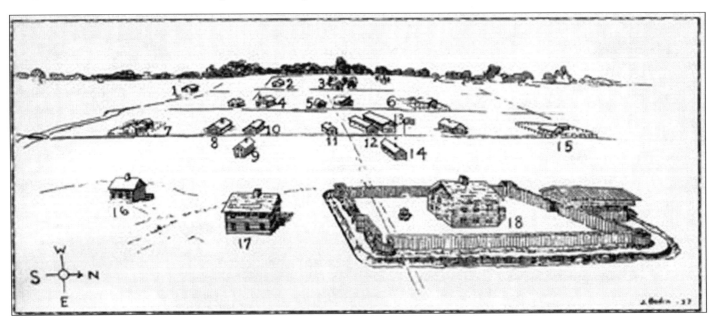

Forest City Stockade map. (Courtesy of the Forest City Stockade)

Forest City Stockade postcard. (Author's collection)

an exact replica and adheres to the original stockade dimensions of 120 square feet with ten foot logs stretching upwards. The cabin at the center of the walled-in fortress is much like the original homestead that protected 240 settlers for ten days in 1862. Filled with authentic artifacts, the cabin is akin to stepping back in time. A Forest City Stockade brochure tells that 1,200 logs were used in building the stockade walls. The restoration construction was done by youth under the NYC program, by the 682 Engineer Batallion of the Minnesota National Guard, and volunteer workers from the area.

Costs of the project were covered almost totally by donation from Meeker County residents. Most contributions were made

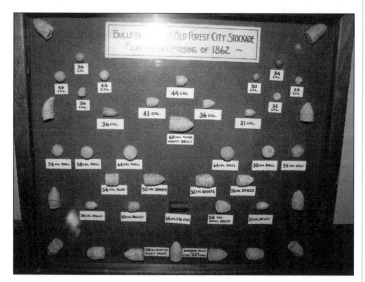

Forest City Stockade bullet display. (Author's collection)

Forest City Stockade model display. (Author's collection)

Forest City Stockade today. (Author's collection)

Above and at right: Forest City Stockade today. (Author's collection)

in the form of the price of one log ($6.40). Today time and the elements have necessitated that the logs be replaced with treated lumber. You can purchase one log for the project for $25.00.

Just outside the stockade walls stands a replica of 1862 Forest City. Built to resemble Forest City as it looked in its earliest years, the dozen or so buildings provide a glimpse of pioneer life in the mid-1800s in central Minnesota, then very much the frontier. Most of the buildings are authentic. Some were just days from demolition. As Bob Hermann, Forest City Stockade board member, and my tour guide for the day, tells that an area resident planned to burn his family's old log homestead on his property. A chance conversation at a Lion's meeting brought existence of the building under notice. After taking a look at it, a committee determined it would be perfect for the village. It was moved to the stockade where it was

Forest City Stockade today. (Author's collection)

repurposed as the chapel. The homestead owner, Lowell (Butch) Engelbrekt, was so honored he made four stained-glass windows for the chapel as well as donating funds to help with the restoration of it. Bob Hermann explained the care and intricacies of relocating and restoring the buildings. Each log had to be taken down, numbered and then transported to the site and reassembled. Some of the building's walls were chinked with stones and rocks embedded in them and the volunteer builders embedded stone chinks as well. A large barn (new construction) was fashioned in the style of the era. It houses an impressive collection of antique farm machinery donated in one large group by a family wanting to keep the collection intact. Again, the donors were so honored they offered funds to help with the barn's construction. The stockade is blessed with donations and talented volunteers that spend countless hours restoring and maintaining the site.

Another building houses a vintage, working printing press. The press operates during the stockade's events and prints special-edition newspapers and prints. Pencil drawings are issued on a limited-numbered series and are becoming collector items. A school house features authentic furnishings, books, desks, photos, and more. Volunteer Gerry Moen plays the school marm during the stockade's annual events. Several volunteers fill roles within the stockade and during its events.

One building houses intricate scale models of Forest City buildings along with several other authentic artifacts. Not only is history recreated at the stockade, it is recycled. Nothing goes to waste. Old logs are saved for re-use elsewhere in the stockade complex. Of course, none of this would have been possible without the concentrated efforts and hard work of volunteers who serve in many capacities from construction to maintenance, creating authentic crafts, foods, and role-playing.

The Stockade is open twice a year. The Rendezvous is the third weekend in August and features authentic crafts and demonstration, horse-drawn wagon rides, tours, presentations, leather crafts, soap making and many foods that include buffalo jerky, fry bread, old-fashioned rock candy and root beer, sweet corn, pickled eggs, and much more.

A Pioneer Christmas is celebrated the first week in December. The wood stoves are fired up and folks can partake in a

19TH ANNUAL PIONEER CHRISTMAS

at the

Forest City Stockade

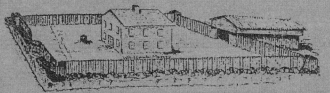

6 Miles Northeast of Litchfield on Highway 24

Saturday, December 6th, 2014
11:00 a.m. - 5:00 p.m.
Admission $3 • 12 & under free

Visit with Santa • Pioneer Crafts
Sleigh Rides • Pioneer Trading Post
Making Old Fashioned Ornaments
Live Christmas Music

See a winter encampment
Tepee • Wall Tent • A Frame

Continue your collection with the
17th piece of Stockade Pottery
and 3rd Annual Print - "Campsite"

- FOODS SERVED ALL DAY -
Cream can stew • Homemade ice cream
Fry bread & Lefse • Coffee • Old Fashioned Rootbeer

Dress Warm | Lots of Outdoor Activities

www.forestcitystockade.org

Pioneer Christmas flyer (opposite). (Courtesy of the Forest City Stockade)

Christmas of the past. The event includes a horse-drawn sleigh ride, Santa Claus, carolers, handmade crafts, *lefse*, homemade stew, homemade ice cream, and hot cider to name a few. The spirit of Christmas comes alive in an authentic setting.

Special tours can be arranged, as can weddings and other events. Take the journey and visit the past. It's as close as you can get to visiting the past. It is truly a unique experience at a genuine historical gem, one you and the entire family can enjoy.

GREENLEAF

1858 - 1906

CLASS D

APPROXIMATE LOCATION:
Just north of County #22 and County #18 junction

Settled in 1856, platted in 1857, Greenleaf didn't see much activity until the mid-1860s due to the Dakota Conflict. When an early settler's ox was killed, supposedly by the Dakota, folks figured it was a convenient time to move elsewhere for a while. The town remained in limbo for three years. When residents returned, the community grew rapidly. The flour mill, built in 1862, had sat idle during the Dakota Conflict, was put into operation. Soon a grocery/hardware, two other general stores and a hotel were part of the community. For a short time, Greenleaf was the Meeker County seat and the Land Office was located there, having moved from Forest City but before it moved to Litchfield in 1869.

Greenleaf store circa 1950s. (Courtesy of the Meeker County Historical Society)

Greenleaf Store today. (Author's collection)

Early Greenleaf Store. (Courtesy of the Meeker County Historical Society)

Greenleaf scool, 2014. (Author's collection)

Greenleaf scool today. (Author's collection)

Greenleaf today. (Author's collection)

Being so close to Litchfield, which had the railroad was the county seat for a time, Greenleaf could not survive. The grocery store was the last business to close. The former store still stands as does the former school building. A few other rural buildings also remain at the former town site.

LAKE STELLA

1899 - 1940s

CLASS D

APPROXIMATE LOCATION:
County Road #33 and County Road #14

While scouting out Meeker County's lost towns, Gerry Moen visited the used-to-be community of Lake Stella. Stopping to take photos of the old creamery, now a private home, Gerry stopped to visit with two women sitting on the deck of the home/creamery taking advantage of the unseasonably warm late September day.

Reminiscing, the women talked about Lake Stella's early days. The little community was platted in 1899 and was located on the border of Darwin and Ellsworth Townships. Lake Stella was sometimes called the Crossroads or Casey after the family that lived nearby.

Orpha Mattsfield, 102 years young, recalled buying dress fabric at the store. Her mother worked at the store. The creamery closed in 1937 when it consolidated with the Darwin Creamery. Dances were held, first at the store, and later in the old creamery building. Orpha also recalled picnics and the Lake Stella band that, at one time, entertained an audience of over 800. A post office was located in the store. Improved transportation caused the decline of the once vibrant community. Today the creamery still stands and is a private home.

Lake Stella Creamery today. (Courtesy of Gerry Moen)

Early Lake Stella Creamery. (Courtesy of the Meeker County Historical Society)

Lake Stella today. (Courtesy of Gerry Moen)

LAMSON

1870 - 1903

CLASS C

APPROXIMATE LOCATION:
County Road #5 in eastern Meeker County

For nearly a year the region had been in the grips of the Dakota Conflict with fear, tensions, misconceptions, injustice, and apprehension rampant. So when two men, out hunting, came upon the two Natives picking berries, their first instinct was to shoot. Not knowing who the Natives were, Nathan Lamson fired at the older Native, wounding him in the hip. Returning fire Lamson was hit and felled. More shots were exchanged, and Nathan's son, Chauncey, fatally shot the already wounded Native. Thinking his father dead, Chauncey returned to town to seek help. Returning to the site, the settlers found the body of a Native, but Nathan's body was nowhere to be found. Upon the men's return to town, the townspeople, including Nathan, greeted them.

The slain Native was determined to be Chief Little Crow. His body was taken to Hutchinson where it was ravaged, badly mutilated and buried in dung. The other Native, Little Crow's son, was captured several weeks later. Nathan received $500 as a reward from the State of Minnesota. Chauncey, who actually fired the fatal shot, collected a bounty for Little Crow's scalp. Today a historical marker commemorates the spot. 109 years after the incident, Little Crow's body was returned, in 1971, to his family and a proper burial was conducted.

Early Lamson. (Courtesy of the Meeker County Historical Society)

108

The town of Lake Todd, actually first located in McLeod County, took the name of Lamson. Businesses included two general stores, a post office, blacksmith, saw and grist mills, and a creamery. One of the stores was called the Glass Box due to its many windows. In 1890, land was donated for the construction of the Swedish Evangelical Church. Struck by lightning in 1911 and completely destroyed, it was later rebuilt. The church was disbanded due to diminishing membership and was torn down. A fixit shop operated in the 1950s. Anderson Seeds operated in the area.

MANANNAH

1857 - 1907

CLASS D

APPROXIMATE LOCATION:
County Road 22 North of Litchfield, West on 355th Street

Lucy Ann Lobdell settled in Manannah in 1856. The New York native was said to be an excellent marksman and had been since she was twelve years old. She could outshoot any man. Lucy Ann dressed in men's clothing and supposedly changed her name and passed as man for two years. Accusing her of impersonating a man, the Meeker County attorney filed charges against her. The court found a woman could wear pants and the case was dismissed. Branded the "wild woman of Manannah," Lucy Ann was ostracized and eventually left town and went back east.

Manannah, one of Meeker County's earliest settlements, was at the heart of the Dakota Conflict of 1862. Fearing for their lives, area settlers took refuge in the area's hotel. Eleven men had sought shelter at the Forest City stockade, and when they returned to Manannah, four of the men were killed. The incident was called the Manannah Massacre and today a marker details the event. In 1863, a stockade was built around part of the town site.

In the late 1800s, Manannah had three general stores, a flour and feed mill, hotel, cabinet shop, two blacksmiths, a barber, creamery, pool hall, and harness shop. Today a few rural-based settlements continue at the old town site.

NORTH KINGSTON

Early 1900 – 1940s

CLASS B

APPROXIMATE LOCATION:
Meeker County Road #24 and Kingston Street

Not to be confused with Kingston which still has a mayor and city organization, North Kingston was a small area set aside in Section 6 of Kingston Township. A privately run creamery operated from 1910 until the

Bird's-eye view of Manannah. (Author's collection)

FEBRUARY 7, 19___

North Kingston Creamery Election

The annual meeting of the stockholders of the North Kingston Creamery was held last week. All of last year's officers were re-elected as follows: G.G. Robinson, president; Matt Leppa, treasurer; Victor Carlin, secretary and manager and Swan Standlund, John Stein, and George Gulso, directors.

Early North Kingston. (Courtesy of the Meeker County Historical Society)

North Kingston Dairy Association was established in 1922. The small settlement also had a grocery store and beer parlor. The beer parlor was made into a home, the creamery is gone and there are few remains of the community.

ROSENDALE

1871 – 1906 (1960s)

CLASS E

APPROXIMATE LOCATION:
County Road #28 just west of County Road #4

Though before her time, Mary Gilbertson remembers her father, John Rogers, talking about Rosendale. During the early 1950s, he operated a tavern in the small community. Later he served as Meeker County's sheriff (1971 to 1987). The tavern is long gone, as are all Rosendale's former businesses, though some original buildings still stand.

The Danielson Creamery, named for the township, was established in 1890. From the beginning it was a focal point of the community. The original building burned in 1917 and was rebuilt. That second building stands today. The community's first store was called the Farmers Store. Many area

Rosendale. (Courtesy of the Meeker County Historical Society)

Rosendale Creamery. (Courtesy of the Meeker County Historical Society)

Rosendale Store. (Courtesy of the Meeker County Historical Society)

Rosendale Creamery. (Courtesy of the Meeker County Historical Society)

Rosendale 2014. (Author's collection)

Rosendale today. (Author's collection)

Early Rosendale street scene. (Courtesy of the Meeker County Historical Society)

Rosendale street scene today. (Author's collection)

residents sold eggs, chicken, and hides to the store. That building also stands today, and if you look closely you can make out the faded "Rosendale" on it. Rosendale did have a mill that ground feed. Residents said the entire town shook when the mill was operating. Another vintage building now serves as the town hall. There are also a few homes in the area.

STROUT

1896 - 1904

CLASS D

APPROXIMATE LOCATION:
County Road #1 and #28

Back in 1985, a young teen from the Danielson Hustler's 4-H club researched, documented, photographed and wrote a history of her home area, Strout. Well-researched and full of history, including maps, that brief history book is a rich document that tells the story of one of Meeker County's lost towns, Strout. In fact, the hand-drawn map helped pinpoint the locations of businesses and buildings long gone.

According to the 4-Her's history and other sources, Strout was named for Captain Richard Strout. Ordered to gather his men and any new recruits he could muster, he was to head to Meeker County in August of 1862. The Dakota Conflict was in its infancy and reinforcements were needed. Marching out with his men and travelling the 160 miles from Minneapolis to Meeker County, the troops often camped in fields along the route. One night the soldiers camped at an open field along the Henderson-Pembina Trail, at the edge of a valley. Having successfully participated in the Battle of Kelly's Bluff, the people of that small village named the community after the captain. The honor may have been misplaced as two years later, Captain Strout's reputation was not favorable, as Bridget Barka wrote, the captain was not prairie nor Indian wise and his military tactics were questionable. So much so, that he was dismissed from service.

Established in 1897, the Star Lake Creamery was the hub of the community, which also included two general stores and two blacksmiths. The creamery's butter was considered among the best and even won awards.

Early Strout store. (Courtesy of the Meeker County Historical Society)

Star Lake Creamery. (Courtesy of the Meeker County Historical Society)

Strout map. (Courtesy of Meeker County Historical Society/Bridget Barka)

Strout today. (Author's collection)

A school lay one mile north of the town center, as was the Lyons Store. Towns often had a main central hub but some businesses, schools, and churches were geographically distant from the heart of the town. The Lyon Store operated until the 1960s. Sandy Johnson and her family purchased the property upon which the store and school once sat. The store stood for many years and was used as a garage by the Johnsons until it burned down. The school is no longer standing. Walking the property with Sandy, we saw the original footprint of the store building as well as the depressions in the land that marked the school's location.

Driving along County Road #1 at the intersection with County Road #28, the former town is now a collection of homes and farms. The Star Lake Creamery, for years, a local landmark, was used for several years as a storage facility, and was torn down when the road was expanded. It stood too close to the new highway. Using Bridget Barka's map, we were able to pinpoint where the old creamery and blacksmiths shops stood, again proving the value of preserving history.

Pope County

Cheesetown store, 1922. (Courtesy of the Pope County Historical Society)

CHEESETOWN

1890s - 1925

CLASS A

APPROXIMATE LOCATION:
Barsness Township

Cheesetown—sounds like a great place for dairy lovers and Green Bay Packers fans. It was established when a group of farmers wanted to build a cheese factory. Area residents Ole and Inga Quam donated one acre of land for a total price of one dollar for that purpose. Things did not go as planned. Even though a building was erected, no cheese was ever produced.

The building later became the Barsness Store (named for the township). The store sold everything—groceries, clothes, shoes, hardware, even furniture—and was run by a succession of owners. Not only was the store the commercial center of the small community, it was the community center as well, hosting dances, weddings, and meetings. It even served as the local polling place and provided employment opportunities for area residents.

An article written in the early 2000s by Rebecca Webb reported that the decades-old, unopened old store safe sat in a home across from the old store site. Tongue-in-cheek, Webb sets the stage for the safe's opening, a la Geraldo Rivera's infamous Al Capone cave opening. In researching the tale, the reporter learned the safe had sat so long in the nearby home it seemed a part of the house. Residents built around the safe until one owner decided she wanted to put shelving where the safe sat. Weighing several hundred pounds, moving it was not an option anyone wanted or looked forward to doing.

Speculation about what was in the safe ran rampant. Guesses ranged from old store receipts to stashes of cash. Options for opening the safe were just as prolific. Everything from blasting it open with dynamite to selling it on Ebay were proffered, including leaving it where it was. At the time of the article, no decision had been made. DARN! I want to know what was in it!

FLINT

1890s

CLASS A

APPROXIMATE LOCATION:
Between Glenwood and Lowry

Short-lived Flint was a rail stop between Glenwood and Lowry. It had a hotel/boarding house and one other building. Little else is known about the community.

GROVE LAKE

1872 - 1907

CLASS A

APPROXIMATE LOCATION:
1 Mile NE of Grove Lake on County Highway 22

Through the years, Grove Lake grew into an active community. Begun in 1870 with the construction of a store, over the years other stores and businesses would join the community. There was a shoe store, blacksmith, and boarding house. A cooperative creamery operated from 1902 until 1925. With the advent of a rapidly expanding automobile travel, an auto repair shop opened in 1922.

Community organizations were an important part of life in Grove Lake. A Woodmans Hall was built in 1895. The building was sold in 1939, and the proceeds from the sale were used to purchase nearly eight acres to be set aside as a park, the Grove Lake Township Park.

An early town band had thirty-five members and a small four-piece orchestra provided entertainment. A literary society was very active. Community events were common and well-attended. They included Fourth of July celebrations, oyster stew suppers and church activities. The Pope County Historical Society tells of one resident's remembrances of the Fountain Medicine Show. The traveling entourage featured a burro and two dogs doing tricks. While not sophisticated, the "medicine" sold at these events made the entertainment seem more lively. It was said to cure any ailment, at least for a while. The good feelings were probably due to the high alcohol content of the "medicine."

Church life was also an important fact of life in Grove Lake. Trinity Lutheran Church and the Grove Lake Methodist Church were among those offering spiritual guidance.

Education was a priority as well. The first school, a log building, was used until a frame building was erected in 1880. The Pope County Historical Society writes that the early schools even offered hot lunches. At first the meals were cooked by the seventh- and eighth-grade girls, but with state aid and commodities later available, cooks were hired. Transportation to and from school on four bus routes was provided by horse drawn busses. Later a so-called "modern" school was built, complete with two classrooms, a library, boys and girls lavatories, kitchen, dining room, cloak room, and a furnace room. Christmas programs and other events were common, and an active PTA rounded out school life. The school was later torn down.

Changing economic factors, and improved transportation caused Grove Lake to decline, becoming a town of the past.

GROVE LAKE ACADEMY

1877 - 1888

CLASS A

APPROXIMATE LOCATION:
Shores of Grove Lake, between Stearns and Pope Counties

Ahead of its time, innovative in its methods and liberal in its approach, the Grove Lake Academy was a true experiment in education. Also known as St. Paul's High School, the academy was located on the shores of Grove Lake between Pope and Stearns County. Established in 1877 by Rev. D.J. Cogan, the school focused on individualized instruction. Students participated in the independent study format and progressed at their own pace, with faculty assistance as needed. There were no set classes and the curriculum offered was a full slate of core courses as well as practical courses including hygiene, bookkeeping, logic and elocution.

Pope County historian Mildred Demonceaux states that tuition was $90.00 for a five-month term. Cogan offered parents a full refund if they were not satisfied with the school. Demonceaux also writes that Charles A. Lindbergh, Sr., prominent Minnesotan and father of the famed aviator, was once a student at the academy.

Destroyed by fire in 1888, it was hoped the school would rebuild. Unfortunately that didn't happen. Rev. Cogan and the school were heavily in debt, and Cogan was at odds with his home diocese. His liberal views at one time cost him his vocational title. Reinstated to the priesthood one month after the fire and reassigned to a parish in Sauk Centre, he died one year later.

NEW PRAIRIE

1872 - 1883; 1920 - 1946

CLASS A

APPROXIMATE LOCATION:
4 Miles SW of Cyrus and ½ mile S of MN 28

Not many towns were named after a wood stove, but local folklore says that the town was named by Gustav Larson after his New Prairie brand of wood heating stove. Others say it was the geographical feature of the region that gave the community its name.

New Prairie store, 1993. (Courtesy of the Pope County Historical Society)

At left: New Prairie street scene, 1993. (Courtesy of the Pope County Historical Society)

Below: New Prairie store interior, 1993. (Courtesy of the Pope County Historical Society)

Pope County's last established village was originally a rail stop along the Little Falls and Dakota Railroad. In an unpublished New Prairie history, Pam Engebretson writes that New Prairie was a railroad town from start to finish. As she tells, the depot created the town, passenger service provided access for commodities and people and opened up markets for products.

Settled by those of Scandinavian descent, primarily Norwegian, the surrounding area was farmland and agriculture played a dominant role in all aspects of life as well.

A varied business sector offered residents nearly everything they could need and included two grain elevators, a bank, post office, blacksmith, livestock yard, lumberyard, and fully stocked general store. Many remember the variety of groceries and the wide selection of goods available, everything from bolts of fabric, dry goods, hardware, and especially the complimentary coffee and cookies. Lutefisk was a specialty item stocked during the winter months, and especially for the Christmas season. Later more stores would join the community, some lasting until the 1950s.

Just north of the village a one-room school provided educational services. Spiritual needs were met by area churches, including St. John's Lutheran Church.

The Dust Bowl years coupled with the Great Depression dealt New Prairie a blow it could not survive. Times were so difficult, Engebretson writes, that without crops to feed their livestock, farmers resorted to using any greens/grasses that they could find, including thistle and tumbleweed. As can be expected, stock did not thrive on the sparse diet. Though severely affected by the hardships of the 1930s, the automobile proved to be the last straw for New Prairie. As people became more mobile and it became easier to travel, New Prairie was bypassed by larger towns and cities that could provide more variety, lower prices and other amenities such as refrigeration, and electricity. After its decline, New Prairie reverted to private property.

Ramsey County

GLADSTONE

1888 - 1923

GLOSTER FROM 1928 - 1941

CLASS A/G

APPROXIMATE LOCATION:
Absorbed by Maplewood in 1957

Nearly every "boom and bust" own shares a common thread, that of being dependent on one industry or one resource. Not so for Gladstone, the Ramsey County community located at the junction of two railroads, was home to not one, not two, but three major industries.

Years before Gladstone was platted and officially established, the three companies were firmly entrenched in the burgeoning community. In 1865 the Lake Superior and Mississippi Railroad and the Wisconsin Central Railroad converged at the site. Platted in 1886, but never incorporated, Gladstone was home to the St. Paul Plow Works, the Ramsey County Poor Farm, and the Gladstone Railroad Shops. Together the three, in the 1890s, employed 1000 workers.

The Gladstone Railroad Shops, located on the southwest corner of Frost Avenue and English Street (Lake Avenue), were used primarily for building and repair of locomotives and other railroad equipment.

The Ramsey County Poor House was one of the oldest in the region. Originally located at the present day Minnesota State Fairgrounds, they moved to a rural area away from St. Paul (near White Bear Avenue) in 1885. Evolving into the Ramsey County Nursing Home, they would later move again.

Building products for farmers (barn wagons, Buckeye Seeders, Sulkey Plows) the St. Paul Plow Works began in 1876. Together the three companies were a solid, established base for a community to grow. Hopes were that the enclave would "rival St. Paul."

By the end of the 1880s, a hotel, boarding house, general store, meat market, at least two saloons, and a brothel called Gladstone home. A school was organized in 1870 and in 1889 opened for a six-month term. Records show that enrollment was such that three employees were hired, two teachers, a male at $50.00 per month, a female at $35.00 per month and a janitor at $5.00 per month. According to Pete Boulay, author of a history on Gladstone, the school had four rooms and was a two-story red-brick building. The school also served as a community center for over sixty years.

Boulay provides a detailed histoy of the afore-mentioned companies. In summary, the Railroad Shops closed in 1941, putting many out of work. In 1949 the Seeger Refrigeration Company (later Whirlpool) leased the buildings. Under the terms of the lease, all the buildings were torn down in 1979, even the landmark water tower. In 1994, the City of Maplewood bought the twenty-four-acre site as open space.

The St. Paul Plow Works burned in 1892. The cause of the fire was never determined. According to Boulay, the company survived the fire but could not overcome a bank failure in 1897. The Works Building sat idle for a few years until 1903 when the Poirier Manufacturing Company began its production of grain drills. In 1907, the owner suffered a stroke and the company went bankrupt. The buildings were vacated in 1921. For years the site was a town dump. During World War II, children scoured and dug the site for scrap metal. Steel was very rare, and extra money could be made by selling salvaged metal. Today, the site is a residential area.

According to Boulay, there were several factors in the demise of Gladstone. Chief among them were The Plow Works bankruptcy and the Gladstone Railroad Shops closing. These businesses were the major source of employment. With no jobs and no money, people resorted to burning their homes for the insurance money. Gladstone, in Boulay's words, "became a ghost town."

In the mid 1920s in order to avoid confusion with Gladstone, Michigan, the community's name was changed to Gloster. The depot stayed open until the 1950s when the auto age began in earnest.

Gladstone would officially cease to be when in 1957 it was absorbed by Maplewood. There are still a few businesses that use the Gladstone name.

Renville County

Beaver Falls, 1910. (Courtesy of the Renville County Historical Society)

Beaver Falls

1867 - 1904

CLASS A/F

APPROXIMATE LOCATION:
Beaver Falls County Park

The stakes were high. Being designated as a county seat could make or break a town. Beaver Falls was one town whose fortune waxed and waned with the title.

Beaver Falls, originally called Beaver and Beaver Creek, was a thriving business and commercial trade center of Renville County. Located just a mile and a half from the Minnesota River, Beaverites (as Beaver Falls residents were called) could boast of a beautiful location, equi-distance from east and west borders, most of the population centered in the area, access to transportation (steamboat), and the hope of a railroad coming through the community.

When Renville County was official organized in the mid-1860s, after the Dakota Conflict, Birch Cooley and Beaver Falls were in a heated contest for the county seat designation. Both had been temporary county seats for a short time. Beaver Falls won that election. However the battle for a permanent county seat would take over fifteen years, from 1885 to 1900.

A booming business sector included a store, hotel, saloon, grist mill, shingle mill, brewery, hardware, bank, three doctors (two of them were a husband and wife team), an attorney, and a ferry. There was also a sawmill, newspaper (the *Beaver Falls Gazette*), and churches. St. John's Episcopal was built in 1891 and a Methodist Church Congregation. A railroad depot was built in anticipation of the expected rail line.

In 1888, Bird Island set about gaining the county seat. Renville and Olivia began to lobby in earnest as well. Campaign goals later changed to making sure Bird Island didn't get the county seat designation. Bird Island would not get it and Olivia helped Beaver Falls celebrate retention of the seat. State law said that another removal election could not be held for four years.

In 1894, Olivia and Beaver Falls were the finalists and an election was ordered. Olivia had set aside land for a courthouse and Beaver Falls had already built a two-story building, which it offered to the county free of charge. Still, Olivia won the election.

Litigation continued and the Supreme Court deemed the results invalid as Olivia did not receive fifty-five percent of the vote. After much debate, Olivia was ruled the new county seat.

Beaver Falls had lost the valuable asset. In 1900 the county seat was moved to Olivia, where it remains today. Residents and businesses followed suit and moved to Olivia as well. In the winter of 1909/1910, St. John's Episcopal Church moved as well. Steam engines were used to carry the structure over the frozen land. The church was active until 1966 when it became a performing arts center. In 1997, the building was moved to the Renville County Museum in Morton.

The railroad did eventually come through Renville County, but not through Beaver Falls. The Hastings and Dakota Railroad took a northerly rather than a southerly route, bypassing Beaver Falls.

With the loss of the county seat and the railroad, Beaver Falls became a part of Renville County history and today is the site of Beaver Falls County Park.

Beaver Falls town hall. (Courtesy of the Renville County Historical Society)

Beaver Falls. (Courtesy of the Renville County Historical Society)

BECHYN

1888 - 1904

CLASS C

APPROXIMATE LOCATION:
10 miles north of Redwood Falls, Near intersection of 735th Avenue and 300th Street

Considered one of the oldest Bohemian communities in the United States, Bechyn was the name for the settlers home community of Bechyn Bohemia. Long before a post office was established in 1888, St. Mary's Church had been built on donated land. Early church services were held in private homes.

In 1904, the town included a blacksmith, two stores, a restaurant, town hall and several homes. Later a gas pump and another store were added. Town activities included dances, picnics and baseball.

In 1915, the present-day church was built. A preservation committee was formed to keep the church from being demolished. All that remains of the community today is the church, parish house, cemetery, and a few homes. Each year the church hosts a Czechfest, complete with polka music, food, and fun.

BIRCH COOLEY

1866 - 1871

CLASS A

APPROXIMATE LOCATION:
Near Morton Minnesota

One of Renville County's first, if not *the* first, communities, was named for the abundance of birch trees in the area. "Couley" or "Coulee" is French for "bed of a stream (even if dry) with steep banks." Several homes, a store and blacksmith made up the town. A fire in 1874 destroyed the town. When the second postmaster moved to Morton in 1882, the post office went with him and was later renamed Morton.

Bechyn. (Courtesy of the Renville County Historical Society)

BROOKFIELD

1897 - 1914

CLASS A

APPROXIMATE LOCATION:
Section 1 Brookfield Township and Section 6 Boon Lake Township

Built on barren land, the Brookfield Store in 1901 offered a bit more than most general stores. They offered the "New Era" automobile, manufactured in St. Cloud, Minnesota. St. Cloud did manufacture Pan Cars, and it is unclear if New Era was a model of Pan or its own entity. The storekeeper also traded horses and bought eggs and poultry.

Employees of the store didn't have far to go to get to work. In the winter, they boarded in the store. In the summer, they pitched tents next to the store. In 1915 the store burned and was promptly rebuilt. Dances, political meetings, picnics, and baseball games were held at the store site. There was also a blacksmith in 1915, with that building being converted to a cow and horse barn/post office combination.

A school was formed in 1905 and operated until 1951 when it consolidated with Buffalo Lake. The property was later sold. Operating two days a week, the feed mills large stationary grinding engines fascinated area children. The store burned again in 1922 and was not rebuilt. Only the creamery well remained in 1981.

Brookfield today. (Courtesy of the Renville County Historical Society)

CAMP

1880 - 1904

CLASS A

APPROXIMATE LOCATION:
Three Mile Creek

When the post office was first established in 1873, the town was called Renville. Later a town of Renville was established, and the name was changed to Camp. Situated along the stage coach route from New Ulm to Beaver Falls, Camp was a convenient stopping place, and the Three Mile Creek Hotel offered a good night's rest. Camp's restaurant and saloon provided for other necessities and respites. A general store/hardware, blacksmith, and grist mill were also part of the community. When the railroad bypassed Camp, the hotel closed in 1877, and Camp itself would fade into history.

Camp today. (Courtesy of the Renville County Historical Society)

CHURCHILL

1890s – 1960s

CLASS A

APPROXIMATE LOCATION:
Section 34 Brookfield Township

Known for its annual chicken pie suppers, Churchill's Methodist Congregation outlasted much of the community. Meeting in private homes in its earliest days, a church was built in 1901. A creamery, general store, a two-room schoolhouse built in 1903, and a Woodmans Hall were the other town buildings. The building was later converted into a township hall when the school consolidated with Hector in 1952. Burned in 1960, a new township hall was built.

Undergoing major repairs and renovations in 1942, the church added a basement with kitchen and dining facilities. Though still standing, dwindling membership forced the church to close.

CREAM CITY

1886 – 1905

CLASS A

APPROXIMATE LOCATION:
Center of Osceola Township

Owing its existence and its name to the creamery, Cream City's only other business was the store right next door to the creamery. There was also a nearby school.

When farmers bought their milk in, they shopped for supplies at the store. Later, a lean-to was added to the store and it was a popular entertainment center. The Cream City Band offered music and dancing. The store burned in 1907, and in 1912 only the school remained. The town band did continue for many years after the demise of Cream City. The region has reverted back to farmland.

Cream City Band. (Courtesy of Renville County Historical Society)

Churchhill. (Courtesy of Renville County Historical Society)

Cream City today . (Courtesy of Renville County Historical Society)

130

EDDSVILLE

1877 - 1905

CLASS A

APPROXIMATE LOCATION:
1 Mile south and 1 mile east of Bird Island

As in many early farming communities, the creamery was the center of activity. So it was in Eddsville. Tired of low prices, the area's farmers established a creamery. Soon 140 patrons and 900 cows were members. During the first month of operation, co-op members received the decent price of sixteen cents per pound for butter fat.

A post office was established in 1877. In 1901 a large general store with living quarters joined the community. Offering a wide variety of goods, the store soon became the social center of Eddsville. Parties, school plays and other events were held in the store. Operating under several owners, it finally burned down. The cause of the fire was determined to be accidently spilled gasoline. The last building in town was torn down in 1978.

Above: Eddsville Store; below: interior of store. (Courtesy of Renville County Historical Society)

Eddsville today. (Courtesy of Renville County Historical Society)

Street scene, Eddsville. (Courtesy of Renville County Historical Society)

FINN TOWN

1860s

CLASS A

APPROXIMATE LOCATION:
1 Mile SE of Franklin on Renville County 5

Finn Town. (Courtesy of Renville County Historical Society)

With a name like Finn Town, it is easy to guess where the early settlers originated—Finland. Arriving before the Dakota Uprising of 1862, the earliest business was a hotel. Unfortunately the owner was killed by the Natives. His wife later remarried and sold the hotel.

Hoping to spur the community's growth, one owner offered to pay passage for anyone from Finland who would come to Finn Town and would work and pay off the passage cost within one year. Many responded and came to Finn Town. Building hand-hewn log houses on the hillside, they also built traditional saunas (Finnish bath houses) into the hill. They were made of stone and approximately twelve feet square. According to the Renville County Historical Society, nature has reclaimed Finn Town. Old logs, cellar depressions, and stones from the saunas are hidden in the overgrown brush.

Above: Finn Town sauna. (Courtesy of Renville County Historical Society) Bottom: F

FLORITA

1886 - 1905

CLASS A

APPROXIMATE LOCATION:
Junction of Renville County Roads 4 & 21

Local residents also referred to Florita as Peanutville, because as folks would gather at the store and discuss the day's news, they ate peanuts, shucking the shells on the floor.

The small community had a post office from 1886 to 1905, a store with a barbershop in the back, and a creamery. The store closed in 1909 and burned a year later. When the creamery closed in 1912 it signaled the end of the town. Florita just could not compete with the expansion of railroad and auto transportation.

A monument to honor the pioneers of the village was erected at the site of the store and creamery.

Florita town marker. (Courtesy of Renville County Historical Society)

HUSKY TOWN

1933 – 1980s

CLASS A

APPROXIMATE LOCATION:
Junction of Renville County Roads 2 & 3

Technically not a town, yet nonetheless the heart of the surrounding community, Husky Town as it was affectionately known, was actually the Barsness Store. Opening in the midst of the Depression in 1933, the store sold a full line of groceries, soft drinks, kerosene, and Husky Gasoline, thus the name.

Electricity had not yet reached the region in 1933, so lighting was by kerosene. In order to keep products cool, ice was cut each year from the Minnesota River and stored for summer use in an ice house behind the store. Things got easier in 1939 when electricity was available. Open from early morning to late evening, seven days a week, the store was convenient for all.

Operating under several owners, the store stayed in business until the 1980s. The Renville County Historical Society tells that it has since burned down.

LAKESIDE

1871 – 1902 (1989)

CLASS A

APPROXIMATE LOCATION:
Boon/Allie Lake

Lasting until 1989, the creamery was the mainstay of Lakeside. In fact, the creamery pre-dated the town. Begun as the Boon Lake Creamery Association in 1897, the name was changed to Lakeside in 1900. For years, butter was the chief product, and it was shipped by team and wagon, by sleigh and by rail to Hutchinson and Buffalo Lake on an ongoing basis. Often a load of coal was part of the cargo shipment.

At left: Husky Town; Below: Husky Town today. (Courtesy of Renville County Historical Society)

Lakeside. (Courtesy of Renville County Historical Society)

Lakeside today. (Courtesy of Renville County Historical Society)

Lakeside's first store began as a tobacco processing business on Lake Allie and later moved to the town site. In order to host community events, dances, school plays, and community meetings such as 4-H, a second floor was added to the store. Structural issues would force the closing of the top floor. In 1930, the creamery burned and was replaced with a new building that same year. When the store closed in 1958, the building was purchased by the creamery and torn down. The creamery closed in 1989.

VICKSBURG

1860s - 1905

CLASS A/F

APPROXIMATE LOCATION:
3 Miles North of Delhi

Settled in the late 1860s, Vicksburg is considered one of Renville County's oldest villages. A post office operated during at least three different time periods between 1871 and 1901. With a general store, wagon shop, sawmill, blacksmith, church, and a ferry to cross the river (where today's bridge now stands) the businesses provided for most necessities. Yet without a railroad the small village was doomed, it was only a matter of time.

That time came when the neighboring community of Renville secured railroad service. Businesses and residents moved to Renville and other nearby communities. When the post office closed, the town of Vicksburg ceased to exist. The last resident was gone by 1905. The First Christian Church was converted to a private home; the cemetery is being reclaimed by nature. The abandoned town site became a county park. The Renville County Historical Society writes that cement slabs from the old town site are visible in the park yet today.

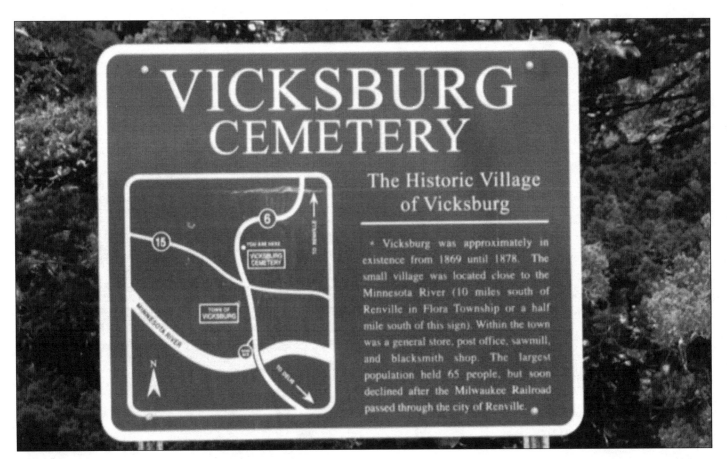

Vicksburg today. (Courtesy of Renville County Historical Society)

Scott County

Helena. (Courtesy of Shawn Hewitt Collection)

BRENTWOOD

1860 - 1872

CLASS G

APPROXIMATE LOCATION:
Absorbed by Jordan

Brentwood may have had very few residents and even fewer businesses, but it did have railroad service and a depot. Surveyed in 1860 and platted in 1898, there were twelve city blocks with 150 lots. A special act of the Minnesota Legislature merged Brentwood with nearby Jordan, to be incorporated as Jordan.

Animosity over the railroad caused tensions between the two, now one, communities. Brentwood had the railroad and Jordan wanted it. When the depot burned, Jordan petitioned to have it rebuilt in their portion of the town, but that bid was unsuccessful. As Brentwood declined and Jordan grew, Brentwood was considered "the wrong side of the tracks." In the mid-1970s the town site of Brentwood was occupied by Martin Homes and the Valley Green Mobile Home Park.

DOOLEYVILLE

1861 - 1870

CLASS A

APPROXIMATE LOCATION:
Location unknown

Usually when a post office is discontinued, postal services are transferred to a nearby larger facility. In the case of Dooleyville, the post office was discontinued in 1870, and Dooleyville was gone. No transfer, no records, nothing, vanished. Named for Samuel Dooley from Indiana, who later became a judge, the town was at the juncture of the Omaha Railroad line and several well-travelled wagon roads.

HELENA

1858 - 1904

CLASS A

APPROXIMATE LOCATION:
Helena Township

Butter was big business in Helena. The creamery had an output of 500 pounds of butter, daily. A general store and sawmill was also located in the town. Little else is known.

JOEL

1897 - 1917

CLASS A

APPROXIMATE LOCATION:
Blakely Township

Joel's store and post office was a multi-purpose building. It also served as a saloon, telephone exchange, and dance hall. A creamery was also part of the community until both the store and creamery closed in 1917.

LOUISVILLE

1853 - 1861

CLASS A

APPROXIMATE LOCATION:
Louisville Township

Laid out in 1854 with wide streets and alleys, and lots of land put aside for public use, Louisville (also known as Yankton for a short while) grew well for four or five years. After the initial burst of growth, the community's thirty homes and few businesses moved to Chaska and other nearby communities.

MUDBADEN

1922 - 1951

CLASS G

APPROXIMATE LOCATION:
1 Mile North of Jordan in Sand Creek Township

Claiming to cure nearly every ailment from rheumatism to hypertension to gout, Mudbaden heavily advertised the curative powers of the region's sulfur springs. Clients, several well-known including, some say, Lucille Ball, flocked to the spas of Mudbaden just to bathe in the mud dug up from the river bank. A two-story brick Classic Revival building is now located on the National Register of Historic Places. The community, first called Lynville, was also a station on the Great Northern Railroad line.

ST. LAWRENCE

1857 - 1901

CLASS A

APPROXIMATE LOCATION:
St. Lawrence Township

Even though cattle were successfully raised on the 1,000-acre piece of land, the land was poor for farming. Still, the owner saw more potential for the property and in 1856 platted it as the town of St. Lawrence. A large hotel, which burned twice, and a home were built there, but not much else. The railroad bypassed the town and sealed its demise.

Sherburne County

Left: Original Bailey station on Sherburne History Center grounds. (Photo taken at Sherburne History Center 2014, by author Rhonda Fochs); Right: Bailey depot photo marker. (Photo taken at Sherburne History Center 2014, by author Rhonda Fochs)

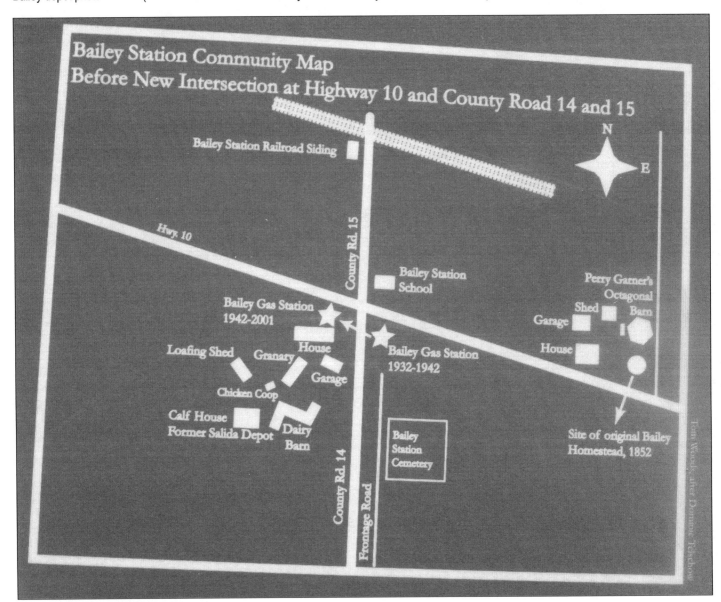

Bailey map marker. (Photo taken at Sherburne History Center 2014, by author Rhonda Fochs)

BAILEY

1887 – 1892 (1950s)

CLASS A

APPROXIMATE LOCATION:
Intersection US Highway 10 and Sherburne County Road 15

Long before Highway 10 became a modern major roadway, it had already long been a transportation corridor for earlier modes of transportation. Serving as the primary thoroughfare for the Red River Oxcarts, later a military road and a stage coach route, communities along the roadway witnessed a lot of history.

According to the Sherburne History Center Library and information plaques on display, in 1852, early settler Orlando Bailey started a farm between Elk River and Big Lake, just east of Highway 10 and Sherburne County Road 15. Fifteen years later, the St. Paul & Pacific Railroad laid tracks one-half mile north of the stage coach and ox cart trail. Bailey, the new rail siding erected at the site, became a community connections point. A school, two retail stores, a cemetery, a school, and a post office completed the settlement. The post office operated under the name of Orlando from 1887 to 1892

For years the school doubled as a church and hosted lectures, debates, lyceums, and township meetings. As automobile usage increased, Bailey was the site of a long-standing service/filling station. That original building is now on display at the Sherburne History Center. Informational placards highlight the region's history with words and photos.

CABLE

1884 – 1892 (1960s)

CLASS C

APPROXIMATE LOCATION:
5 Miles South of St. Cloud on Highway 10

Today, the old truck stop stands sentinel over the former Cable town site, most of it now under Highway 10. In its earliest days, the town consisted of two railroad depots, one for the Great Northern the other for the Northern

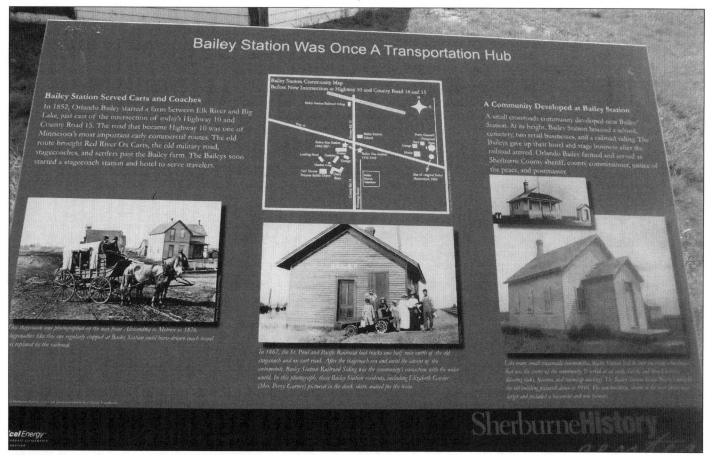

Bailey Station marker. (Photo taken at Sherburne History Center 2014, by author Rhonda Fochs)

Pacific, a horse-powered grain elevator, a stockyard, store with a dance hall on the second floor, and the Cable Congregational Church.

The church, established in 1887, was active for many years. In 1920, the church building was sold to the Haven Township Board for $450.00, the amount the church owed in debts. The building was used as a town hall and meeting space until the 1950s when the construction of the new Highway 10 necessitated its removal.

Cable Depot (at left). (Courtesy of Shawn Hewitt Collection)

Cable Truckstop circa 1960s (below). (Courtesy of Elaine Paumen); At bottom: Cable Truckstop today (Author's collection)

PALMER

1874 - 1885

CLASS A

APPROXIMATE LOCATION:
West side of Briggs Lake

The community consisted of a post office (under the name Briggs Lake) and a store. The Elcor Resort was a popular spot, and it is said Lawrence Welk played there.

SALIDA

1880s

CLASS A

APPROXIMATE LOCATION:
Intersection US Highway 10 and County Road 11

For decades a filling station has stood at the crossroads of US Highway 10 and County Road 11. The first, owned by the Mitchells was torn down at the second expansion of Highway 10, and a newer, larger station was built. There wasn't a rail stop at the site, but trains would stop if flagged down. Primary shipping commodities were lumber and farm products. Today, a gas station still stands on the northwest corner of the intersection as well as a few other businesses.

WHEELER

1874 - 1885

CLASS A

APPROXIMATE LOCATION:
East bank of Mississippi River, 7 miles below Sauk Rapids

Several building lots were sold, but no buildings were ever built. The town never developed.

Sibley County

BRACK

1899 - 1903

CLASS A

APPROXIMATE LOCATION:
8 miles north and 1/5 mile west of Gibbon

Built on the dream of a railroad coming through the area, the town of Brack (pronounced brake) was short-lived. The post office lasted only four years. Several families in the area were Ahlbrechts and the 1898 plat shows no less than six farms owned by an Ahlbrecht. In the local history book *Bits and Pieces of Sibley County History* a grand-daughter of the Ahlbrechts recalled that her grandfather owned 1,000 acres of land and gave the land to his sons. The community's creamery was started by the Ahlbrechts; the boys even had a band at one time.

The *Bits and Pieces of Sibley County History* book also tells the tale of Ida Ahlbrecht, as recounted in an Ahlbrecht family history. I have summarized and paraphrased Ida's story.

Near the turn of the century, Ida was a very young child, perhaps seven or eight years old. One day, Ida went out to the field where her older brother was mowing grass with horses and a sickle. He had stopped and asked his sister to hand him the oil can. To reach the can, she had to step over the sickle and that movement signaled the horse to start again, and, tragically, Ida's leg was cut off. Blood was squirting everywhere. Putting his sister on the seat of the mower, her brother drove home as fast as he could run. By the time they reached the house, Ida had fainted. People didn't call a doctor in those days, they made do. So they bandaged Ida up, but there was so much blood in the house, they moved her to the hay in the barn. Moving her to the hayloft, to escape some of the flies, she lay there, alone, all night. Her father said she would be dead by morning. Ida later said she didn't sleep much due to the pain.

The next morning, Ida's brother went up to the hayloft and the two looked at each other. He went back down and, when asked if she were still alive, he said, "Yeah, she looked at me." Her mother tore up a bedsheet and rebandaged her leg to help with clotting. They left her in the barn and on the third day unwrapped the bandage and saw the maggots. Her bone was sticking out and her father said that her leg would never heal like that. So he and Ida's brother, held her leg down and sawed off the bone, stretching the skin over the end. Ida later said she didn't scream as "Father was Father and you just didn't fuss around him." When Ida was in her teens, she came upon a man with an artificial limb. She inspected it, and, when she got home, she went out in the grove, found a log and whittled and carved her own artificial leg. Up until this time she hopped around on her good leg. It is said that Ida loved to dance, especially to polkas and waltzes.

DOHENY'S LANDING

1857 - 1862

CLASS A

APPROXIMATE LOCATION:
Jessenland Township

Originating as a river boat stop, the community's post office was called Jessenland (supposedly after the local name for Jessie's Land). As early as 1854, a warehouse and a store opened near the boat landing. After the railroad was routed across the river, Blakely became the area's trade center. The warehouse was moved to a spot near an area farm where it was remodeled and used as a home until it was razed in 1911.

FAXON

1852 - 1901

CLASS A

APPROXIMATE LOCATION:
Faxon Township

First called Walker's Landing, then Big Hill in 1857, and lastly Faxon when it was platted in 1859, the settlement was one of Sibley County's earliest. Around 1862 there was a ferry to a site in Scott County, which later became known as Murphy's Landing.

The 600-acre town site established post offices as Big Falls and Faxon. Soon several businesses were active, including three general stores, a blacksmith, two saloons, a steam-powered saw mill, shoe shop, hotel, and livery. A warehouse was built near the boat landing. The settlement was a major wheat shipping center in 1866.

HARTFORD

1857

CLASS A

APPROXIMATE LOCATION:
8 Miles southwest of Henderson

Hartford, on the Fort Ridgely Road, was also known as Freemont but since another Minnesota town had that name, it had to be changed. The area was incorporated in 1857, but there was no real development.

MOUNTVILLE

1862 - 1902

CLASS C

APPROXIMATE LOCATION:
Transit Township

Fleeing their New Ulm home during the Dakota Conflict of 1862, the Uber family settled in the Mountville area and operated one of the town's two hotels as well as the livery stable and store.

St. Michael's Church was built in 1872 and was later abandoned when the congregation moved to Gaylord in 1882. The town's skimming station and spinning wheel factory were the last businesses in operation. Today, the Sibley County Historical Society has a photo showing a model of the spinning wheels made in Mountville.

Mountville church today. (Courtesy of Sibley County Historical Society)

Mountville church. (Courtesy of Sibley County Historical Society)

150

NEW ROME

1856 - 1902

CLASS C

APPROXIMATE LOCATION:
Kelso Township – 4 miles from Arlington

Early travelers thought the area a good resting spot. Leaving behind the River Valley where trees were common, the land now opened up to prairie. The area was so scenic Warren Upham wrote that the community was considered the resort area of Henderson. The Fort Ridgely Trail had been developed in 1852 with the intent to provide easy access to the proposed military fort. It was a military man, Captain John Groetsch who first settled in the area, and he became known as the founder of New Rome.

The settlement began as Prairie Mound, but the postal service complained there were too many towns with "prairie" in them so it was renamed New Rome.

Church services were held as early as 1864 and were conducted under the wild plum and cherry trees. In 1869, St. Johannes/St. John's Evangelical Church was built on that very spot where those early services had been held. It wasn't long before that first church was too small and a new forty-by-eighty-foot one was built, as was a school, parsonage, and a cemetery platted.

The community grew and soon included a blacksmith, church, and dance hall, and plans were in the works for a wagon shop, harness shop, and furniture store. A farm implement dealer lasted from 1918 to 1920. Several social groups were active, including the baseball team and Cornet Band. Lobbying for the county seat designation, New Rome was thriving. Unsuccessful in the county seat bid and with nearby Henderson becoming a bustling river port with its natural crossing place, New Rome began to fade. The last straw was the railroad bypassing the town. St. John's Church was disbanded in 1956, and the building was razed in 1957.

New Rome postcard. (Courtesy of Sibley County Historical Society)

New Rome today. (Courtesy of A. Filer)

RUSH RIVER

1862 - 1903

CLASS C/G

APPROXIMATE LOCATION:
Kelso Township, later merged with Le Sueur
South branch of the Rush River

Some traditions are best put aside and forgotten. Rush River's Fourth of July anvil event was one of them. Hoping to create a bit of hoopla and excitement for the celebration, blacksmith Charlie Christianson put a load of black gunpowder under his anvil. He then lit the gunpowder to see how high the resulting explosion would lift the solid steel anvil. Human nature being what it is, and people wanting bigger and better, more bang for the buck (quite literally in this case), more and more gunpowder was added. The custom came to a halt when an extra-large layer of gunpowder was used. The anvil went up and came down on the blacksmith's leg. Then and there the custom ended. The next year, Charlie sold the blacksmith shop.

Settlers first began arriving in the area in the 1850s and the first school was built in 1858. An itinerant preacher provided spiritual services, and in 1882 land was donated for a church. That church later merged with the Tabor Church in Le Sueur in 1946, and the church building in Rush River was sold and torn town. Consolidation with the Le Sueur school district closed the Rush River School in the 1950s. The community also had the nickname of "Euchreville" because of the residents' passion for playing the card game Euchre. The town hosted Euchre tournaments.

Established in 1900, the creamery building burned to the ground shortly after opening. The second creamery building, constructed of wood, was moved to a nearby farm in 1935 when a brick creamery was built. The new creamery operated until 1970.

In the 1970s all that remained was the old creamery and store—operating as the Tri-Ag Services—several homes, and the cemetery.

Stearns County

FREMONT

1857 - 1864

CLASS A

APPROXIMATE LOCATION:
Just south of Clearwater, on the right after I-94 overpass

As I learned about Minnesota's lost towns, I was awed by how many of them I had driven through without even knowing it. Fremont City is one of the ones I'd been to and never realized it until now. Many years ago, I took my mother to lunch at a café/restaurant near her rural Clearwater home. The restaurant called Brigitte's was just south of the I-94 overpass in Clearwater. Little did I know that we were having lunch in the old town of Fremont City.

Straddling both sides of the Clearwater River and in two counties, Wright and Stearns, Fremont City, purportedly named for the 1856 Republican candidate for office, John Fremont, was one of many towns during that time period named with a variation of Fremont. Another community, Fremont near Silver Creek, is one example and does lead to a bit of confusion.

Platted in 1857, lots sold well for a while. However, few people actually settled in the community. Since Fremont City had been platted and organized as a municipal corporation few people were a problem. The requirements for a municipal corporation state that some form of government be established, and Fremont City had barely enough residents to do so.

An early dam on the Clearwater River powered at least two sawmills. Both were successful, but there were also many nearby successful mills which produced an overabundance of lumber. A flood destroyed the dam in 1868, and another burned in 1870. The mills, however, continued to operate long after Fremont City failed as an organized city in the 1860s.

While the mills were successful, little else in Fremont City was. Unable to pay taxes for many years, in the late 1850s, Fremont lost its incorporation status. Stearns County, in 1863, took possession of the property, then later sold it for less than twenty dollars with the stipulation that the new owner pay the back taxes. The town site was officially vacated in 1864. The mills existed until the late 1880s. The last mill, a three-story structure was moved to nearby Clearwater. An area historian tells that they must have done it during the winter as the steep banks would have made a difficult job nearly impossible at any other time. The mill owners also had problems with the question of water rights—who owns the water going over the dam? Determining water rights was an ongoing issue for many communities.

A 1985 *St. Cloud Times* news article states that the last structure to be removed from Fremont City was the Fremont Bridge. Taken out during construction of County 45 in 1972, area residents found timber foundations and an old iron cog from the mills.

I drove by the old town a while back. The barren land was for sale, ready for new owners and new memories.

GEORGEVILLE

1863 - 1953 (1990s)

CLASS A

APPROXIMATE LOCATION:
Just off Highway 55 between Belgrade and Regal (4 miles from Belgrade)

Garbage was everywhere and so were the rats. The vermin-infested buildings were in shambles, the roofs caved in, and the brick walls crumbling and disintegrating, causing a safety hazard for all, especially the young children who loved exploring the ruins. Things in Georgeville were certainly a far cry from its earlier days.

Originally located in Kandiyohi County (*see* Kandiyohi County for Georgeville's early history), for twenty-six years. Completely uprooting their community, the townsfolks moved the buildings to Stearns County in 1886. Begun in the 1860s, Georgeville was an agriculture-based community. Farming had its ups and downs, and the rural economy fared well enough through tough times. Georgeville, for several years, was a thriving community and supplied the area farmers and residents all the staples they needed. In 1919, an area farmer built a forty-by-eighty-foot brick building, which housed a large general store. Well-built and of high-quality construction, the building served the community for decades and was considered a local landmark. Sadly, the building and Georgeville would fall prey to fringe elements and the seamier side.

While Kandiyohi County had been a dry county, Stearns County had no such restrictions and limitations. In the 1920s and 1930s, Georgeville developed a reputation, with good reason, as a place to go for dancing, drinking, gambling and an all-around good time. A brothel was operating in the town until the early 1960s. Saturday nights found the town packed to the limits with cars parked everywhere, even down both sides of Highway 55, creating all kinds of problems.

The bank closed in 1928 after overextending itself, and the brick grocery store closed in 1953. Then came the hippie phase. In 1961, sixteen young people from Minneapolis moved into the old brick building. They had learned of Georgeville from a Minneapolis realtor who told them of the town and the building. Calling themselves the Stone Age Industries, the hippies would, on occasion, reluctantly sell their handmade crafts, leather goods, and other items to raise money for their necessities. Living communally, they also had a small plot of land for a garden on which they hoped to grow all the food they needed. Quite an unusual situation, gawkers, news media and the curious came to Georgeville to see the "hippies" in real life. After four years, the hippies left town.

After the hippies' departure, an ex-convict moved into the brick building. He had hopes of building a half-way house for other ex-cons and also a pancake house. Neither materialized. Collecting a great deal of machinery and other things (junk?), the owner held an auction in 1975 and moved out of town. Georgeville's last business, a bar, burned in 1981.

The brick building and other buildings, already decrepit, deteriorated even further. By the late 1990s, the roofs were caved in, people complained, and with garbage strewn all over, rats were rampant. The crumbling walls were dangerous, and the entire town was a safety hazard. Stearns County officially declared the buildings a public health hazard and slated them for demolition. Demolition day was in early 2000. Due to threats, a sheriff's deputy was on site for the day. Without incident the buildings were demolished. Local news reports told that the bank vault's walls were one foot thick concrete. In addition to the bank building, a burned-out service station and old store foundation were razed and filled in. Georgeville, in all its glory and largesse, was no more. Today the town lives on in the stories and tales told. Residential homes now occupy the former town site.

LOGERING

1880 – Early 1900s

CLASS G

APPROXIMATE LOCATION:
Absorbed by Eden Valley

The folks of Logering put a high value on the peace and quiet of their small community. Originally called Papplebusch, German for "stand of popple trees," the town later took on the name of August Loegering (different spelling), the settlement's storekeeper. Six foot, six inches tall with a full beard, Loegering was an imposing figure. The German immigrant had first tried farming, but, not liking it

and not very successful at it, he opened a general store in 1880. Soon other businesses followed and included a saloon, diner, butcher shop, feed store, a few homes, a livery, and the Popple Bush Catholic Church. The Wirtshaus & Saloon offered food, drinks, four rooms for rent, and a livery and stable where horses and buggies could be rented.

When, in the mid-1880s, talk of a railroad coming through the area became a distinct reality, the residents of Logering strongly opposed the notion of the railroad changing their community. They put a high price on their land to stop the railroad's progress. Negotiations for the railroad to route through the small town proved fruitless. Undaunted, railroad officials were well-aware there was plenty of land in the area that could be had for a much more reasonable cost. Realizing the value of a railroad coming through the area, a nearby farmer offered to donate land for a right-of-way as well as a considerable amount of land for for a town site. Too good to turn down, the railroad accepted the offer and ran their tracks one-half mile south of Logering. Two miles down the tracks a new village, Eden Valley, sprouted up.

Within a few short years, Logering's businesses and residents moved to the new community, and Logering became a town of the past. There are no remains of the town, except for the bar in Eden Valley's Corner Bar, which came from a Logering business.

MAINE PRAIRIE

1856 - 1919

CLASS A

APPROXIMATE LOCATION:
4 miles north of Kimball on Highway 15

The settlers from Maine had heard tales of the rich farmland in the area, and when they finally arrived in the mid-1850s, they knew they had found the place to call home. Those first years were hard work and filled with trials. In 1856 and 1857, a plague of grasshoppers ate everything in sight. Arriving in hordes, resembling a black cloud, the grasshoppers would descend and finish off all the crops in just a matter of days before moving on. Fear and tensions from the Dakota Conflict necessitated the building of a fort in the area. Constructing a log, forty-square-foot stockade, the fort provided safety, but it was never attacked.

In 1867, after ten years of initial settlement, the building of homes and lives, the village was established. Formally known as Maine Prairie, the residents called it Maine Prairie

Maine Prairie marker. (Author's collection)

Corners or just the Corners. With the usual collection of small community businesses—a blacksmith, cheese factory,

general store, lodge hall, and several civic organizations—the town even had access to a traveling doctor.

When the Soo Line Railroad built their line four miles to the south of Maine Prairie in 1886, the town was dealt a death blow. The post office closed and most businesses, buildings and all, moved to the new town, Kimball or Kimball Prairie, rapidly growing along the rail route. Maine Prairie's last building burned in 1919, and all remnants of the town, except for the cemetery, vanished.

In 1949, a granite marker was erected at the old town site. Replacing an earlier wooden memorial, the granite marker still stands today along Highway 15, north of Kimball.

PADUA

1850s - 1980s

CLASS C

APPROXIMATE LOCATION:
7 Miles south of Sauk Centre at intersection of Stearns
County Roads #22 & 192

Hundreds of thousands of Irish left their homeland during the catastrophic potato famine years of the 1830s and 1840s, including sixteen Rooney families from County Galway. Settling first in Canada, eight of the families moved to Minnesota after the enactment of the 1862 Homestead Act. Spending their first year in Minneapolis, the next spring they traveled to Stearns County where they filed

Hopper dozer. (Commons Licensing)

Padua pub. (Unknown)

Farming and agriculture were important to the area. Inundated with clouds of hungry grasshoppers during the mid-1870s, the pests caused major damage to the crops. All means and methods were used to combat the insects, some quite unorthodox and expensive. Records tell of one method, a machine called the HopperDozer. The horse-drawn apparatus pulled a trough filled with tar. The grasshoppers would be forced into the machine, and then would be blended into the soil. The mashed insects were good fertilizer but the pricey contraption eliminated a minute fraction of the grasshoppers. Things looked so hopeless that in April of 1877, Governor Pillsbury proclaimed a day of prayer and fasting. Shortly after that, the grasshoppers left for good. Coincidence?

In 1924, a Montana cowboy was taking cattle by train to the stockyards in St. Paul. When he got to Brooten, he decided to quench his thirst. He was well on his way to being totally inebriated when he decided he wanted to dance. A resident offered to take him to Padua, where a dance was being held. Once he got to Padua, his drunken behavior was so obnoxious the ladies refused to dance with him. Not liking the rebuff, the cowboy left the hall only to return with six-shooters drawn. A local news article of the time wrote that he forced the dancers to crawl on their hands and knees. Proceeding outside, he began to shoot out street lights and anything else he could find. Eventually overtaken, he was arrested, jailed and sentenced to three months.

Padua was always the social center of the area and still is. Annual events were always well-attended and included a St. Patrick's Day Parade and celebration complete with green beer and Irish stew. An Octoberfest event, a fall festival, and a Cinco de Mayo meal, as well as many dances and events, kept the town lively. A Padua Reunion was held in 1982. Today the town's only business, the Padua Pub, owned for years by Rooney descendants, still keeps the spirit of Padua lively. Lisa Lenarz, the Rooney's daughter, tells that the pub is open 365 days a year, including Thanksgiving and Christmas Day, for those who don't have anywhere else to go on the holidays. Rooney descendants Dave and Clara Rooney explain that the pub is located in the old grocery store. The Catholic Church was closed in the early 2000s and now operates as a House of Prayer, with set hours and on-going prayer times.

When the railroad routed through Brooten, Padua abandoned plans to incorporate, and the village declined. The pub and church still stand.

homestead claims on four sections of land near the small community then known as Getty Grove. In 1857 John Getty had settled in a heavily wooded area nine miles south of Sauk Centre. The settlement became known as Getty or Getty Grove, and it included a school, post office, store, blacksmith, creamery, and the first Catholic Church in the region, Assumption Catholic Church. A visiting priest conducted Mass once a month.

The Rooney settlement, was also known as Rooneyville, Rooney Station, and Irish Landing. The Assumption Church in Getty Grove had closed, and the building was moved to the Rooney area where it was used as a school and later a granary. As Rooney grew, Getty Grove declined, and soon Rooney was the burgeoning area. Rumors were the railroad was expected to route through the settlement, and the rumor fueled the community's growth.

In 1897, a wood-frame church was built in Rooney. With a large, ethnically diverse population, the pastor did not want to show any favoritism to any one group, so he named the church after the patron saint of Italy, St. Anthony of Padua. The town soon adopted the name Padua. When the wood-frame church burned to the ground in 1943, it was replaced with a red brick structure that still stands. A parish hall, used for weddings, receptions, town meetings and for voting purposes was built in 1952.

The Padua School was organized in 1870. In the early days, the school was so poorly equipped that students had to carry their chairs from home each day. As things improved, the school's coal-burning system was replaced with a gas furnace, new desks and books, and running water was installed. Annual events were Christmas programs and the end-of-the-year family picnic. The school consolidated in 1970.

Padua had two general stores, two public halls, two creameries, four saloons (at least one of them a blind pig), a blacksmith, feed mill, and meat locker.

ST. ANNA

1884 - 1930s (2000s)

CLASS E

APPROXIMATE LOCATION:
7 Miles NE of Albany on Stearns County #9

The black ribbon of roadway winds its way through the heart of today's St. Anna. Back in 1933, when the road was first proposed, it too also went through the heart of the small community. In fact, the road would cause the demise of the Village of St. Anna.

Beginning as a Polish settlement in 1880, near Pelican Lake, religious services and Mass were very important to the primarily Catholic community. The nearest Catholic Church was in Avon, seven miles away. By the mid-1880s, the settlers wanted their own church, and the parish of the Immaculate Conception Church was formed. A wood-frame church was constructed in 1887. In 1902, the building burned to the ground, and the present brick building was erected. By 1890, a general store stood next to the original wood-framed church. The store sold groceries and hardware, and bought eggs and cream from area farmers. A small bar was also located within the store. A second general store operated in the community for a short time. A post office existed from 1884 to 1905. Lasting for decades, the two-room, grades one through eight schoolhouse consolidated with Holdingford. Secondary students had been going to Holdingford for years.

A long and extended legal battle raged in St. Anna in 1912. Susanna Spitzhak alleged that her neighbors, the Reginecks, had lured twenty-two of her turkeys into their coop. The Reginecks claimed innocence. Argued by four lawyers, the case went to trial in St. Cloud. The judge ruled that the Reginecks had not stolen the turkeys, that they were, in fact, theirs. Spitzhak dropped off an appeal, and the case went to the higher court, where the first decision was overturned. Now the Reginecks appealed, and the case was placed on the Supreme Court docket. Determining that since Spitzhak had only dropped off her appeal and had not personally delivered it as the law required, the district court's decision was reversed. The end result, the Regineks got the turkeys. *St. Cloud Time*'s reported Mike Moran concluded that the real winners in the legal brouhaha were the turkeys. Due to the extended legalities, they lived through Thanksgiving, Christmas, Easter and beyond. Legal costs far exceeded the $25.00 value of the turkeys.

Immaculate Conception Church, St. Anna. (Author's collection)

Streets of St. Anna. (Author's collection)

St. Anna today. (Author's collection)

St. Anna, 2014. (Author's collection)

During the Prohibition years, moonshiners were very active in all of Stearns County, including the St. Anna area. The store's bar had moved to a nearby barn where it continued to operate, albeit under cover. The many stills in the area, supplemented the area's economy.

In 1933, Stearns County proposed a new road through the community. Since the village was incorporated and had been since 1915, St. Anna's residents would be responsible for the costs to maintain the road for the one and one-half miles it ran through the village. To avoid the ensuing high taxes, officials dissolved the village, making it part of St. Anna Township. Local residents feel that, not only did the road issue change St. Anna, but so did the changing character and make-up of the community. The end of Prohibition also changed the community as the moonshiners closed down their operations. As the population shifted from a primarily farming community to more of a lakeside style of life with those interested in the recreational aspects of the lake, the focus of the community changed to a more urban makeup. While traffic increased through St. Anna, and a convenience mart and gas station were built, the only other buildings were the tavern and the church. Folks still say they are from St. Anna, and although you can attend Mass in St. Anna, stop for gas or a drink, the village of St. Anna no longer exists, not as a town but more of a crossroads hamlet.

STILES

1900s – 1920s

CLASS A

APPROXIMATE LOCATION:
Ashley Township

Primarily a farming community, Stiles's only businesses were agricultural based and included a grain elevator, stockyard, a depot, and a nearby school. The Little Falls to Morris rail line's engine was affectionately called "Little Dinky." Farmers, housewives, and students used the train, which left at 9:15 A.M. and returned at 4:30 P.M. daily, as a commuter train. Traveling to Sauk Centre, it provided easy access to shopping and for students to get to school.

The train was not always reliable, often getting stuck for days at a time in the deep snow drifts. One resident recalled a time when the train was stuck for six weeks!

Both the elevator and the depot burned in 1913. Neither were rebuilt, and the town disappeared. In 1978, a home was being built on the former town site.

UNITY

1890 – 1908

CLASS A

APPROXIMATE LOCATION:
8 Miles south of Sauk Centre

Built with the best of intentions, Unity banked its livelihood on the hope that the Soo Line Railroad would route through their community. In anticipation of becoming a railroad trade center, the community had a co-op creamery, bar, blacksmith, and a grocery store. One-half mile from town, a former school moved in from Lake Henry and was used as the Unity Lutheran Church until 1925 when a new church was constructed. In 1964, the congregation was dissolved.

Unity's hopes for the railroad routing through their community were dashed when the railroad changed routes and gave birth to the town of Elrosa. Unity's grocery and blacksmith moved to the newly created community in 1908, and by the 1930s Unity had disappeared.

Stevens County

GAGER'S STATION

1870s

CLASS A

APPROXIMATE LOCATION:
West of Morris, on County #28

Preparing and planning, at least as much as possible, the settlers from St. Lawrence County in New York, hired a land agent and had him scout out the best locations for their proposed settlement. Selecting prime land in Becker County, Minnesota, the agent sent word that the settlers could travel to their new homesteads. After a series of transportation mishaps, the group finally arrived at the pre-selected sites only to find squatters living on the land. With no other choice, they moved on. Some settled in Otter Tail County, and three of the group went further south to Stevens County and established Gager's Station. Others from New York joined them. Originally called Potosi, meaning "great riches," the postal station was Stevens County's first. Simply a two-by-four-foot box with a few pigeon holes, the "post office" was later used as a cupboard and eventually was on display at the Morris Historical Museum. Nothing remains of the community.

MOOSE ISLAND

1891 - 1908

CLASS A

APPROXIMATE LOCATION:
Halfway between Donnelly and Herman

Farming and the railroad, as well as the Barrett Ranch played major roles in the history of Moose Island. The first building in the town was a section house and was later followed by a lumberyard, coal and wood sheds, and a grain elevator. A post office was established in 1891 and was primarily used for handling mail to the Barrett Ranch. The ranch was owned by Theodore Barrett, a Civil War general and largest landowner in the area. It is said there were many well-attended dances and parties held at the ranch.

The first elevator was horse-powered, and had no scale. The grain had to be hand-shoveled into the hopper. That elevator was later moved to Herman. Moose Island's second elevator was gas-powered and had a scale. Even though there was a station house, there was no depot, just a platform. Passengers had to flag the train down if they wanted to board.

Not so for James J. Hill, president of the railroad. He had his own siding in Moose Island where he often parked his private rail car. Edna Mae Busch, Stevens County historian, tells that Hill liked to hunt at nearby Neimachl Lake in Grant County. Supposedly it was the only place with trees for miles. Nothing marks the spot today.

165

Swift County

Fairfield today. (Courtesy of Andrew Filer)

FAIRFIELD

1873 - 1907

CLASS A

APPROXIMATE LOCATION:
Section 5 Moyer Township

Owing its existence to its location along the stage coach route from Appleton, Fairfield established a post office in 1873. The small community also included a blacksmith shop, general store, and a creamery.

With time, railroads became the transportation mode that built America. As the railroad routes were planned out and the double steel tracks laid out, the fate of many towns and communities was decided. Progress and prosperity would come to those lucky communities along the routes and decline for those places bypassed by the railroad.

Unfortunately, Fairfield was one of the communities no longer easily accessed by transportation routes.

The new rail line running from Benson to Appleton gave rise to two new trading centers, one being Holloway. The Fairfield shopkeeper moved his general store to the newly created community, and soon Fairfield, as a town, would cease to exist.

Fairfield area today. (Courtesy of Andrew Filer)

Traverse County

BOISBERG

1901

CLASS A

APPROXIMATE LOCATION:
Minnesota side of the Bois de Sioux River across from
White Rock, South Dakota

Planned as a residential extension to White Rock, South Dakota, Boisberg was on the Minnesota side of the Bois de Sioux River. The town never developed.

CHARLESVILLE

1904

CLASS A

APPROXIMATE LOCATION:
West of County Road 9 adjacent to County Line

Never incorporated, Charlesville was platted in 1904, adjacent to the county line, just west of County Highway 9. Originally Charlesville was on an old stage coach line, and later on the Great Northern Railroad line. In 1987 an elevator and small grocery store were all that remained.

COLLIS

1885 - 1954

CLASS A

APPROXIMATE LOCATION:
Us 75 South from Wheaton
Just North of County Road 4

Reminiscent of Tara Hill in Ireland, Collis was named by a village priest, from the Latin for "hill." The name is fitting as Collis was on the highest point above sea level in Western Minnesota.

Settled primarily by Irish homesteaders, the town, platted in 1900, was along the St. Paul, Minneapolis, and Manitoba Railroad line. A small community, the town consisted of the church, a blacksmith, two groceries (one with a dance hall on the second floor), a post-office, and several residences.

An early mail route originated in Collis. Nearby Dumont had

turned down the route as the merchants in Dumont believed their town would garner more business if people had to come to town to get their mail rather than having their mail delivered to their homes. Later mail deliveries would depart from Dumont.

DAKOMIN

1916 - 1917

CLASS A

APPROXIMATE LOCATION:
12 Miles from Wheaton on T149 shore of Lake Traverse

Combining the names of the two states sharing its border was the early transportation hub of Dakomin. In the early 1900s the Great Northern Railroad put in a spur line from Browns Valley to the head of Lake Traverse where Dakomin was located. At that same time, the Lindquist brothers installed a barge service on the lake. Hauling primarily grain, an elevator was soon built for storage. A general store, post office (from 1916 to 1917), and several residences completed the community.

One day in 1913, the elevator caught fire while loading grain onto the barge. The Traverse County Historical Society states that the fire was most likely the result of an overheated gear box igniting the chaff. The barge service was discontinued in 1917, and the unincorporated town declined and eventually faded from the landscape.

MAUDADA

1881 - 1884

CLASS A

APPROXIMATE LOCATION:
On the Shore of Lake Traverse, just south of the mouth of
the Mustinka River

With panoramic views of Lake Traverse, backed by a wooded ravine complete with a clear, cold spring, Maudada was situated on, arguably, one of the prettiest spots in the region. Platted in 1881 by Washburn and Earsley, the two combined the first names of their daughters and called the community Maudada. Operating with post offices under the name of Lakeview (1878 to 1879), Round Mound (1879 to 1882) and lastly Maudada from 1882 to 1884 the community was off to a vibrant start but had a brief existence.

Rumor had it that the newly proposed rail would be routed through Maudada. Many businesses were started including a forty-five-barrel flour mill, hotel, blacksmith, general store, livery stable, and the *Traverse County Tribune* newspaper as well as several residences.

The race for designation as county seat was hotly contested. Election results in 1881 had Maudada eking out a sixteen-vote margin of victory over Browns Valley. Browns Valley strongly protested the election results. In addition, a crafty plan to sway sentiments was put into action. As the *Wheaton Gazette* states, Browns Valley asked for a stay pending a contest. Judge Brown ordered court to be held in Maudada. Some in Browns Valley had an idea. Browns Valley, was the nearest rail station to Maudada. When the respected judge arrived by train in Browns Valley the night before the court proceedings, he was given the finest room in the hotel. The judge was afforded royal treatment, a grand meal, and the best of everything Browns Valley had to offer.

Early the next morning, the judge boarded a rickety old wagon and was taken on an arduous, roundabout way over the roughest and longest route possible. Then the full-bodied judge arrived in Maudada, four hours later, he found a small, barely furnished room that served as the court house. The only accommodations were a nearby farmhouse, filled to capacity with the very large farm family. Judge Brown was indignant. He immediately adjourned the court to be reconvened the next day in Browns Valley. Thus ended Madudada's reign as county seat.

Officially the courts deemed the county seat election as null and void, some say fraudulent, as Maudada was never incorporated. It appears the election results were problematic as well. Maudada voters must have been very eager as the community's twelve voters cast no less than thirty votes.

With the county seat designation gone and the proposed railroad line routing through the newly established community of Wheaton, Maudada would cease to exist as a town. Buildings were torn down or moved. Soon nothing remained but depressions left by caved-in cellars.

Washington County

Mower House, 1800s. (Courtesy of Arcola Mills Historic Foundation)

ARCOLA MILLS

1846 – 1910s

CLASS C/H

APPROXIMATE LOCATION:
12905 Arcola Trail N., Stillwater, Minnesota 55082

Layer by layer, the history of Arcola Mills unfolds, revealing the true archeological gem that it is. Arguably, it's the most significant and important site along the St. Croix River, if not the entire state of Minnesota. In fact, it can be argued that Arcola Mills supplied the white pine that built Minnesota and points beyond.

Arcola Mill's heritage is preserved, and its legacy maintained and sustained by the Arcola Mills Historic Foundation, a non-profit group of dedicated community and stewardship-minded individuals.

Archeological evidence shows that centuries before Europeans settlement, the area was inhabited by Native peoples as far back as ancient times and long before the Woodland period or the Dakota and Ojibwe years.

The white pine era constitutes the next layer of Arcola Mills history. Husband and wife, John and Garcia Mower, along with John's brother, Martin, came to the area when it was still wilderness, with wolves and plentiful game. John Mower served in the Territorial Legislature as well as the state legislature. Mower County (though pronounced differently) was named for John Mower. The brothers built an impressive Greek Revival mansion in 1847. The home afforded a scenic view of the river and was surrounded by woods and creeks. It is said to be the third oldest and largest totally timber framed house in Minnesota.

Garcia Mower was a key figure to the settlement. She served as hostess for visitors and was the center for social life in the community, and she also saw to the settlers' welfare, in addition to managing the trade with the area's Native people. Martin founded the historic Boom Site between Arcola and Stillwater. Several boats in the area were named for Garcia. Arcola was truly a Mower family affair.

A sawmill was built in 1844/1845, and a settlement grew around the mill. While the location of the Mower House, the blacksmith shop, and one of the mills is definitely known, the locations of the other town entities are educated approximations. In a 2004 article, Cathy Clayton states that the 1857 census approximates the village's location as "a band one mile deep . . . along the St. Croix shore from one mile south to five miles north." Because of the wood pilings at the river's edge, it can be assumed the warehouse and store were located nearby. She continues that the village began when the Mowers opened a general store for their neighbors, their employees, and the residents of a nearby small community across the river called Little Canada. Operating until 1865, the store was joined by blacksmith and carpentry shops. Clayton states that there were eleven significant structures. The community was also home to a wedge factory and a steamboat building facility.

Though platted, the town was never recorded. In 1859, Clayton writes, a school was established. A new school building was constructed a few miles northwest of the mill in 1868. The school building still stands on its original site on Highway 95 and is now a private home.

In addition to the advantage of the river, the location was an ideal site for the mill because of the area's several streams and springs. Encompassing a fifty-six-acre site, the settlement was called Arcola Mills and included a general store, school, blacksmith, and other businesses needed to service and supply the mills and the town residents. A "boxcar" depot was located near the intersection of Highway 95 and the tracks. The river served as a highway for settlers and for the timber industry. The community operated a farm, which supplied the residents with dairy, grains, and vegetables. For years, the booming village thrived, until the early 1900s. Several factors combined to cause the demise of Arcola Mills. By 1917, the timber had been overcut,

Mower House, 2005. (Courtesy of Arcola Mills Historic Foundation)

Mower House, 2005. (Courtesy of Arcola Mills Historic Foundation)

and demand for lumber declined. The coming of the railroad also played a role in the community's decline. The railroad meant that the river was no longer the main mode of transportation for lumber and other commercial ventures. The growth of nearby Stillwater as a commercial, transportation, and government center contributed to the end of Arcola Mills, the town. Within a short time, houses and buildings were moved or abandoned, and the settlement had few remnants. It was, in all respects, a ghost town. The remaining buildings, including the Mower House fell into disrepair and ruin.

Stillwater physician Henry Van Meier and his wife, Katharine, were early herbalists. They often walked the region's rural areas in search of plants and ferns. One day as they were walking in the woods along the St. Croix River, they happened upon the decrepit remains of the Mower House. Immediately falling in love with the building, the Van Meiers knew they had to rescue and restore the once majestic home. Using it as a three-season

home, the Mower House and the scenic grounds were stunning.

Katherine, by all accounts, was flamboyant, vivacious, effervescent, eclectic and fun. Originally from Virginia, her family had been involved with advancing local arts and artisans. In fact, she and her family were key figures in the emergence of the Craft movement. Katherine's brother-in-law was Sherwood Anderson, famed for his great influence on the art of short-story writing. His style and content influenced a generation of authors, including William Faulkner. Anderson was also instrumental in Ernest Hemingway's first published works. His social group included the likes of Gertrude Stein. Katherine carried the love of art and the support of artisans to her new home in Arcola. She surrounded herself and her home with artists, writers, and other eclectics, who would stay for extended visits. This included Anderson and Stein. The couple moved in several cabins to house their guests and they hosted artists of many and varied disciplines. The compound was referred to as an "artist colony."

Mower House, 2005. (Courtesy of Arcola Mills Historic Foundation)

Sawmill. (Courtesy of Arcola Mills Historic Foundation)

Dr. Van Meier died in 1979, and Katharine could not keep up the maintenance of the large home and grounds. In 1990, she closed the house up and moved. She died in the early 1990s and left the property to the non-profit group.

The Arcola Mills Historical Foundation took responsibility for the home and grounds. Efforts to raise money were successful and are on-going. It is the group's dream to restore the mill site as well. Weddings, receptions, and other events are held at the Mower House. The house and grounds are also open for tours several times during the year. The home and site are simply a must-see for their natural beauty, architectural style and historic significance. Restoration efforts are ongoing, and volunteers and supporters are always appreciated. Full color photos and more information can be found at http://arcolamills.org. Check the website for dates, times, and special events. Call ahead to schedule group tours or to arrange private events.

BIG LAKE

1920s - 1930s

CLASS A

APPROXIMATE LOCATION:

Always a popular vacation area, it is said that even John Dillinger and other St. Paul gangsters hid out at various resorts in the Big Lake Community in the 1920s and 1930s.

In its earliest days, the Red River Oxcarts cut through the Northwoods roughly where Mayberry Trail runs today. A small Swedish settlement had a store and a school but never developed as a town.

DACOTAH

1841 - 1850s

CLASS A/G

APPROXIMATE LOCATION:

With less than an ideal location, the proposed town site did have some assets: a steamboat landing, water power for mills, a level building site and good travel access for carts and wagons. It was a location Joseph R. Brown could make into his dream community.

The first settlers arrived in 1841, and all of them were relatives of Joseph R. Brown, including Dr. Christopher Carli, who was the first, and the only, doctor north of Prairie du Chien. Building a cabin out of tamarack logs, they plastered the walls with mud to keep out the elements, primarily the cold. Calling it the Tamarack House, it became a handy stopping place.

At the time, nearby Stillwater was primarily swamp land but that would change, and Stillwater would become the destination of choice. With few settlers choosing Dacotah, and the increasing competition from Stillwater and Prescott, Wisconsin, Joseph R. Brown's dream community ceased to exist.

GAREN

1890s - 1960s

CLASS A/G

APPROXIMATE LOCATION:
Grey Cloud Island

While Garen itself is long gone something permanent originated in the community, Toni Home Permanent Company, that is. Begun in 1941 by Neison and Irving Harrison, the multi-million-dollar business home was in the former Garen School, which had been closed in the mid-1930s. Toni was later moved to St. Paul and was sold to the Gillette Company in 1958 for twenty million dollars.

The switch-line community was created by a lawsuit settlement with the Northern Pacific Railroad. Area historian Elsie Vogel tells that Garen came into existence when a spark from a passing train ignited a grass fire, which in turn set a nearby peat bog smoldering. The fire caused area farmers great distress,

Toni Home Permanent. (Author's collection)

and they in turned sued the railroad. Agreeing to build a switch yard with cattle pens that would help ease loading cattle into boxcars, the community of Garen grew around the yard. The railroad also moved in boxcars to serve as a station and named the station "Garen" after one of the affected farmers. Soon the community included a store, grocery, and variety stores, and a school, which also served as a community center.

Folklore has it that the Garen area was a favorite spot for Chicago gangsters. Rumor says that Ma Barker rented area cottages as did others. It is a fact that lots of home brewing and bootlegging went on in the region with area dirt roads leading the way to St. Paul for deliveries.

The school operated from 1893 until 1934, when students were bussed to Forest Lake. Records show that in 1898 there were thirty-four students enrolled.

As transportation improved, area roadside establishments became popular stopping places. One of the best known was the Halfway Inn or Happy Landing.

With the completion of Interstate 35, which connected Forest Lake with the Twin Cities, the commute was faster and easier. Forest Lake became a bedroom community, and Garen became a place of the past.

GREY CLOUD

1857 - 1863

CLASS A

APPROXIMATE LOCATION:
Grey Cloud Island

Pre-dating European settlement in the area, Grey Cloud Island was home to Native populations as early as 100 B.C. Archeological evidence confirms the presence of Natives long before the Europeans arrived. The area was occupied by Woodland Mound Builders from approximately 100 B.C. until 600 A.D. and the Mississippi Culture in 1000 A.D. It is said the area has the largest concentration of mounds in the country. In the early to mid-1800s, forty families of the Mdewakanton Band lived on the island.

Stipulations in the Treaty of 1837 required that the Dakota vacate the island and move to Pine Bend in Dakota County. Chief Medicine Bottle and his band left behind their bark houses. The lodges didn't stay empty for long and were soon occupied by the newly arrived fur traders. Many of the men, employees of the American Fur Company, had wed Native women and soon arrived on the island with their families.

The townsite was platted in 1856 by Joseph R. Brown. Advertising heavily, the promoters touted such amenities as a large store, brickyard, blacksmith, steamboat landing, and an unsurpassed view of the river. Hopes were high for the settlement of the town. For whatever reasons, few settlers took advantage of the offer. The Financial Panic of 1857 sealed the demise of Grey Cloud. A dam was later built at Hastings, and that would raise the level of the river. Parts of the old town site were submerged.

LANGDON

1871 - 1933

CLASS A/G

APPROXIMATE LOCATION:
Now Cottage Grove

As the Chicago, Milwaukee, and St. Paul Railroad extended its line from St. Paul to Hastings, two communities developed, one being Langdon. Due to its prime location along that new rail line, Langdon quickly became a thriving community and trade center. Soon an elevator, feed mill, hotel, three stores, a blacksmith, non-denominational church, confectionary, school, and an 1873 Catholic Church were located in the town.

Platted in 1871, the town was named for Bruce Langdon, the railroad builder and later a state senator.

Most of the businesses fell prey to the Great Depression. Also, constructed in 1933, the Territorial Road introduced the automobile age. Shipping preferences changed from rail to trucking, and station towns felt the economic impact. It was more than Langdon could withstand. The post office was closed. The Washington County Historical Society writes that the former Catholic Church was moved to St. Paul Park where it was used for small shops. The school closed in 1955 and, in the late twentieth century, housed the 3M Company Union Hall. Several support groups also used the meeting spaces. The once popular Majestic Ballroom housed an auction house.

East Cottage Grove and Langdon merged to become a "bedroom" suburb. Many housing developments, primarily Orrin Thompson, in the 1950s through the 1970s, made the area residential. Cottage Grove the city eventually absorbed Langdon and the township. Future plans call for a proposed Red Rock Commuter Station to be built on the Langdon town site. Once again, Langdon will house a rail service.

POINT DOUGLAS

1850 - 1866/1866 - 1903

CLASS A/G

APPROXIMATE LOCATION:
West Side of Lake St. Croix

One of the regions earliest settlements, Point Douglas, was also the county's first post office. In fact, it was the first post office in Minnesota to be located outside of Fort Snelling. Point Douglas's prime location, on the west side of the mouth of Lake St. Croix and on the point of land between the lake and the Mississippi River, was a natural stopping place for travelers. Almost immediately after people began traveling through the area, a settlement grew.

The first log home was built in 1838, followed by a mercantile store in 1840 and the post office, transferred from Wisconsin Territory. Since so many travelers stopped at the community, the store quickly became a major supplier of goods needed for settlement in Minnesota's interior outposts. The Union Hotel joined the community in 1843. Classes were held in a private home until a log school was built in 1950.

The Washington County Historical Society states that the town was platted in 1849 and named for Senator Stephen Douglas, who was a moving force in the formation of the Minnesota Territory.

Thriving in 1858, the lumber and supply community consisted of a church, two general stores, the post office, a blacksmith, two hotels, four warehouses, a ferry service, and fifteen to twenty homes.

Point Douglas was always overshadowed by Hastings, which had rail service, and Prescott, Wisconsin. Unable to compete with the growing communities, Point Douglas would, by the turn of the twentieth century, cease to exist.

VASA/OTISVILLE/COPAS

1857-1860/1886-1914/1906-1927

CLASS A/G

APPROXIMATE LOCATION:
Highway 95 on the West side of the St. Croix River

Honoring their Swedish heritage, the early settlers of the town named it in honor of Swedish King Gustav Vasa. At least that was the hoped-for name. However, when the pioneers met, they chose the name Otisville after a

Early Copas. (Shawn Hewitt Collection)

prominent citizen. Organized in 1858, the town actually began in 1849 with the operation of a hotel called the Vasa House. The hotel was the halfway point on the road from Taylors Falls to Stillwater and enjoyed a steady business. A sawmill, store, post office, and saloon completed the community. Done in by the Financial Panic of 1857, the post office was discontinued in 1860.

Later another settlement arose adjacent to the Vasa townsite. Begun by an Italian immigrant, the name Copas is unique and doesn't exist anywhere else. A store was built in 1854. The Washington County Historical Society states that the town developed very slowly until the railroad came through in 1886. Potatoes were the mainstay of the community. Reports state that over 100,000 pounds of potatoes were shipped each year. As transportation trends changed, trucking became the shipping method of choice. With rail service on the decline, Copas passenger train service was discontinued. In 1963, the depot was moved out and the last building was demolished. By 1970, nature had reclaimed the bulk of Copas. The one remaining structure is the Copas home. Built in the 1880s it stands along Highway 95.

WITHROW

1890 - 1963

CLASS A/G

APPROXIMATE LOCATION:
Border of May and Oneka Townships
County Road 9

Built as a railroad station town along the Minneapolis, St. Croix and Western Wisconsin Railroad, Withrow was at its peak in the early 1900s. The community included a creamery, blacksmith, general store, bank, elevator, feed mill, stockyards, lumberyard, potato warehouses, and a pool hall. The post office operated until 1963 and a rural post office until 1966. Withrow was formally absorbed into Grant in 1996.

Wright County

ALBION

1858 - 1887

CLASS A

APPROXIMATE LOCATION:

From the very beginning to the very end, the three Holmes brothers were the mainstay of Albion.

Platted in 1856, lots were quickly sold and bills were introduced into the Minnesota Legislature (in 1857 and 1858) to incorporate the small community. For reasons unknown, the town never took off, and incorporation couldn't save it. The brothers never abandoned the town. They continued to stock some store goods for the convenience of area residents and also managed the post office and a half-way house. When the area experienced a ginseng boom, Albion served as the trade center. During the Dakota Uprising, most area settlers fled to Monticello. A few rode out the scare with the Holmes brothers in Albion. The area eventually reverted to farmland.

ALBRIGHT (ALBRECHT'S MILL)

1900 - 1902

CLASS A

APPROXIMATE LOCATION:
4 miles north of U.S. 12 on Wright County Road 5 on North Fork of the Crow River

Growing quickly at first because of the grist mill, dam and bridge built in 1879, the community lasted only a few years. A creamery, general store, blacksmith, and several residences surrounded the mill. Today the area is a county park.

AYDSTOWN

1850s

CLASS A

APPROXIMATE LOCATION:
Juncture of Crow and Mississippi River

Just across the river and the county line and at the juncture of the Crow and Mississippi rivers, lay two settlements, Dayton of Hennepin County and Aydstown of Wright County. Platted by John Ayds in 1855, a few homes were quickly built. Sure that his town site would be a success, Aydt waited for the influx of settlers to arrive. Unfortunately, they never showed up. Most of the new arrivals to the area chose Dayton, which offered a variety of businesses and services. The Financial Panic of 1857 sealed the fate of Aydt and his town.

CZECHSTOHOWA

1880s - 1900s

CLASS A/C

APPROXIMATE LOCATION:
Franklin Township

Originally part of St. Peter's Catholic Church in Delano, the predominantly Polish community built a church of their own, christening it St. Mary's of Czestochowa. There are many variations and spellings of that name.

The first church was struck by lightning and burned to the ground in 1913. An all-brick building was constructed in 1914 and the active church still stands today. No longer predominantly Polish, many of the area's residents can trace their roots back to the original fifty families that settled the area. In 1984, the parish celebrated their 100th anniversary. A celebratory Mass, catered dinner, and open house drew over 300 people. The guest speaker was U.S. Senator David Durenberger.

Many of today's older residents remember the settlement that grew up around the church, especially the store.

DICKENSON

EARLY 1900s

CLASS A/F

APPROXIMATE LOCATION:
2 miles southeast of Buffalo on Highway 55 (1.5 miles southeast of the junction of Highway 55 and County Road 14)

When I was younger, much younger, we used to save our empty plastic milk bottles so that we could fill them with the cold clear spring water at the artesian well at Dickenson Springs. Every couple of weeks we would load the empty jugs into the car and drive off to fill them. We weren't the only ones filling up with water; there was always someone filling their jugs, even in the middle of the winter. In the winter, the walk to the small metal pipe protruding out of the ground was slippery and treacherous as the continually running water created quite an ice coat. I can still taste the cold water.

While we took turns filling the jugs, I noticed a wooden marker at the spring site. Reading it, I paid little attention to what it said, but then most young people don't pay much attention to old markers and even less to old history. Now, that I'm older and have more history of my own, it's fascinating.

Dug in 1916 by Thomas Dixon, Dickenson Springs, as it was called, was always a popular stopping spot for travelers, who were always welcome to have a drink of the water. The watering hole was just a quarter mile from the Soo Line station town of Dickenson Spring. The depot was a converted box car. The community consisted of a creamery, a variety of stores, and several homes, as well as a brick kiln that shipped bricks almost daily by rail. In the early 1900s a creamery and store were added. Population in 1915 was fifty.

An unpublished manuscript by Myers and Jameson of the Wright County Historical Society tells that there was a string of robberies at the town's creamery. Hoping to quell future thefts, a guard was posted. The sheriff, while doing some investigating, was mistaken for the thief, shot and killed by the guard.

During the droughts of the early 1930s, the spring went dry in 1934. Constructing a wayside rest at the site in 1948, Minnesota Department of Transportation crews accidently struck the protruding well pipe, and the water began to flow again. It's still running to this day.

The wayside rest just to the south of Highway 55 with the railroad tracks abutting, still offers travelers clear cold water. A small parking lot adjoins a wooden historical marker, routed and painted by Glen Dixon, a son of the well's original owner. It was erected at the site in 1989. It informs the reader:

> Thomas Dixon had this well dug on his farm in 1916. It went dry during the drought of 1934. Minnesota Highway Department equipment struck the pipe while building Highway 55 in 1938. It started flowing again.
>
> The ghost town of Dickenson, which was located ¼ mile east of here, was a station of the Soo Line and had a pop. of 50 in 1915. It was named for pioneer Amos Dickenson on whose farm it was located.

ENFIELD

1850s - 1954

CLASS A/D

APPROXIMATE LOCATION:
1 mile east of US 75

Settled by Swedish immigrants in the mid-1850s, Enfield is two miles south of Hasty. Once a busy little burg, the farming community was located along the rail lines

Enfield, 1910. (Courtesy of Dean E. Abrahamson)

through the area. The post office was in operation from 1910 to 1954. As auto traffic increased, small communities, like Enfield, began to decline. The completion of I-94 further eroded the community's base. Today, a few homes, an original building or two are still standing in the former town site. Along I-94 is a spacious rural rest area which carries the Enfield name. A short distance away is the former town site.

Enfield, 2014. (Author's collection)

186

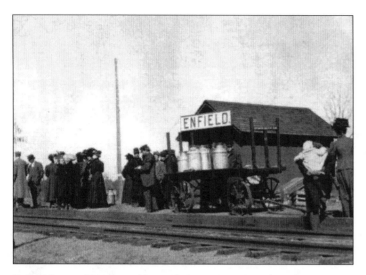

Enfield Depot. (Courtesy of Dean E. Abrahamson)

Enfield train station. (Courtesy of Dean E. Abrahamson)

Greetings from Enfield. (Courtesy of Dean E. Abrahamson)

Berning Mill, Frankfort. (Courtesy of Travis Bonovsky)

FRANKFORT (ON THE CROW)

1856 - 1857

CLASS A/G

APPROXIMATE LOCATION:
Bend of the Crow River near St. Michael

Still a scenic spot along the Crow River today and very popular with canoeists, the former town site is known as the Berning's Mill site. Long before the mill was built, the seemingly popular location for town sites was chosen for three different platted towns. The northernmost one being Franklin (on the Crow). Platted in 1857, there was a store as early as 1856, Franklin Township's first. The store operated until 1865, after which time it was given up and the land reverted to farmland. Later, Bernings Mill was built on the former town site.

Berning Mill, Frankfort. (Courtesy of Travis Bonovsky)

FREMONT

1856 - 1903

CLASS A

APPROXIMATE LOCATION:
Near Clearwater, at the site of the former Brigette's Restaurant, just past and west of the I-494 overpass

Political sentiments more than likely played a role in the naming of the town. The Republican candidate for president in 1856, the time of the town's founding, was Fremont. In 1856, the town's named was changed from Silver Creek to Fremont. (There was also another Silver Creek in the area.) Alas, the town would suffer the same fate as the presidential candidate, defeat and relegated to a few notes in the history books.

Platting a 100-acre piece of land, the developers had plans for a store, hotel, and school. A small steam-powered sawmill had been built at the mouth of Silver Creek. Lots were selling fast, and the mill was producing shingles, laths, and doing edging work nearly non-stop. Things were looking prosperous, but a falling out among the owners would doom the venture. Questions arose as to who legally owned the property, and the arguments that ensued were heavy and lengthy. In 1858 only one of the owners lived in the village, in the hotel. Very quickly, the hotel became the only building left standing. By 1915, the former town site had reverted to farmland.

FRENCH LAKE

1856 - 1903

CLASS A

APPROXIMATE LOCATION:
French Lake Township Section 15

Many settlers traveled along the Territorial Road on their way from Monticello to Forest City and to points beyond. Few stayed in the area. Thus was the plan for Belgian immigrant Ernest Howard. According to D.J. French's early history of Wright County, Howard and his family were on their way to Forest City driving a team and wagon rented in Monticello. Along the way the wagon broke down. Stopping to check the damage, Howard unhitched the rented horses from the wagon, and the animals promptly headed back to Monticello. The family was left stranded without shelter or much food. Making matters worse, an early snow storm set in, and the family was forced to build a log cabin for shelter. The family decided to winter at the cabin and continue their journey in the spring. Twenty-five years later, the Howards were still at that original cabin site. There were tough times for the family the first few years until the ginseng buyers came to the area. The Howards made enough money selling ginseng that they could pay off their land and then some.

More settlers arrived in the area in the late 1850s when the St. Paul, Minneapolis, and Manitoba Railroad ran a line just south of French Lake. During the Dakota Uprising of 1862, the site was nearly deserted, with residents seeking shelter in Monticello, still others went to the Twin Cities and never returned.

In the early 1900s, French Lake was a bustling community and included a creamery, bank, blacksmith, barber, store, a school with two teachers, a church, flour and saw mills, and a temperance hall. A post office operated from 1860 until 1903, and was established four times within that time frame.

Area historian, Lillian Barby wrote of an area farm wife walking to French Lake to trade eggs, buy groceries and mail a letter. When she was finished grocery shopping and wanted a stamp, the storekeeper told her she couldn't trade eggs for stamps. So she returned home without mailing the letter. Two of her young sons were out picking wild raspberries and found enough to sell for two cents (the price of stamps in those days). The woman then walked back to French Lake and mailed her letter.

French Lake experienced many good and some hard times. Grasshopper plagues, diphtheria epidemics, traveling medicine shows, tent meetings, fire, basket and pie socials, ball games, picnics, and school programs were just some of the town happenings.

HASTY

1881 - 1980s

CLASS A/D

APPROXIMATE LOCATION:
Just east of County Road 8 NW and 150th Street NW intersection near Clearwater

Lasting well into the late twentieth century, the small hamlet of Hasty began over one hundred years ago on early settler Warren Hasty's farm. The railroad routed through the area in 1881, and in 1888 a depot was constructed. Residents from nearby Silver Creek wanted to name the station "Silver Creek." They thought the name would serve as a waypoint for travelers who might not otherwise know about their town. That bid was not successful, and the town became known as Hasty.

Early Hasty. (Shawn Hewitt Collection)

Former Hasty Business. (Author's collection)

The Hasty post office was established in 1899 and was discontinued in 1954. A first post office in the area had been established in 1887 as Lund and lasted just a year. The community itself was active far beyond the post office years. For a short while, in 1890, a brickyard was in operation and was said to ship out three or four carloads daily. In 1903 a creamery, hardware and telephone exchange joined the growing community. Soon after, a lumberyard, restaurant, and Community Hall (Sonsteby Hall) were active as well. In 1891

Hasty today. (Author's collection)

190

Hasty remnants. (Author's collection)

Hasty streets 2014. (Author's collection)

a non-denomination church offered spiritual services and lasted well into the 1950s.

Potatoes were the crop of choice, and Hasty was known for almost daily shipments during harvest time. Fire destroyed the lumberyard in 1907, but quick action saved the rest of the town.

Hasty was so busy a full-time dentist and doctor's office existed. Two brothers served as dentist and doctor.

For years Hasty was home to businesses that were landmarks in the area. The Hasty Cheese Shop had a long history. Originally established in 1929, the Modern Co-op Cheese Company was primarily a wholesale operation. The building was enlarged in the 1930s and 33,000 pounds of limburger cheese was made a month. In 1953, government regulations stiffened and wood vats were no longer allowed. It was too expensive to switch over to stainless steel vats, and the recipes could not be adapted to the new process, so the new owners continued selling, not making, cheese. This they did for nearly forty years. People came from far and near to buy the wide variety of cheeses, with longhorn being the biggest seller. Literally dozens of cheese flavors were available, by the round, block, brick, and smaller quantities. Sausage, ice cream, crafts, cold pop, and more were available. A picnic table was supplied for a snack or lunch on the go. With the construction of I-94, traffic patterns changed, and the owners, ready to retire, decided to close the shop in 1975. After a few years of sitting idle, new owners opened the cheese shop in the 1980s. Called the Milky Whey Cheese Shop, they too offered locally made sausages, cheeses, locally made hand-dipped ice cream cones, jellies, jams, and more. The store has since closed.

The Hasty Inn was also a local landmark. Originally a bank, then a produce, feed and seed store, it later became a tavern.

Hasty school, District 13. (Courtesy of Dean E. Abrahamson)

First called the "Try-Me-Inn" it was renamed the Hasty Inn when new owners purchased the building in 1953. The new owners updated the building. even transforming the upstairs into a dance hall. Local country and western bands played nearly every night. In the late 1970s the pool tables were removed and the building was refitted as a grocery store.

Today, a few buildings remain, the Hasty Inn building still stands, though no longer operating, and a few homes still preserve the town and the community. Just down the road, and over the I-94 overpass is the Hasty Truck Stop. Opening in 1976, it is now a convenience store/gas station and restaurant. Lining the walls of the restaurant are vintage photos. Green highway signs still point the way to Hasty.

Hasty business district. (Author's collection)

KNAPP

1897 - 1906

CLASS A

APPROXIMATE LOCATION:
Nessel Township

Following the rail line into the Cokato area, the Swedish settlers were united in nationality and faith. Early church services were held as soon as the first house was built in 1868. Deciding as a community in 1870 that a church was needed, a congregation was organized and plans were made for the building of a church. Shortly thereafter, the North Crow River Lutheran Church was built. Lasting until 1881 when the original church was sold, a replacement was built in 1882. A parsonage was added the next year. A brick building was built in 1902, and that church lasted into the late 1900s. Services were in Swedish until 1925, when English services were offered on a scheduled basis. In 1960, the church congregation celebrated the 100th anniversary.

The community's log cabin school was built in 1872 and replaced with a one-room school house in 1887. At that time the school term was just eight weeks. Increasing attendance necessitated that another room be added to the school and with that came a longer school term, six months. By 1947 the school year was nine months. The school was last used in 1971.

A general store was built in 1894 and the post office operated from 1897 to 1906. A creamery association was formed in 1900, a blacksmith, ice house, and a second general store completed the now gone community.

MANHATTAN

1857 - 1858

CLASS A

APPROXIMATE LOCATION:
Monticello Township just downriver from Monticello

We may never know for sure exactly where the town of Manhattan was located. Records indicate that there were several buildings on the site located just downriver from Monticello. The town ceased to exist in 1858, and no trace remains

MAPLE GROVE

1850s

CLASS A

APPROXIMATE LOCATION:
West side of Lake Sylvia

The only record found is a plat that informs us that Maple Grove was located on the west side of Lake Sylvia and a near a tiny unnamed lake. The tiny lake may have dried up as it does not appear on today's maps. Nothing else is known of the community.

MOUNT AIRY

1850s

CLASS A

APPROXIMATE LOCATION:
Shore of Lake Mary

Traveling along an old trader's trail, the group of claim hunters picked out a possible town site. Less than ideal, the swampland by the shores of Lake Mary was chosen by the group to be that of Mount Airy. On their way back to Rockford, the group stopped for the night at a logging camp. There the men met with tragedy. According to Myers and Jameson, a falling tree killed one of the men and permanently injured another. The proposed town site was killed as well. There is no further mention of it in the records although Rockford township residents did refer to the area as Mount Airy.

MOUNT VERNON

1850s

CLASS A

APPROXIMATE LOCATION:
Near Silver Creek

Touted in advertising as a great location with lots of water power and as a good location for a dam, the small community was just east of Silver Creek. A sawmill was supposedly active for many years.

SMITH LAKE

1869 - 1935

CLASS A

APPROXIMATE LOCATION:
3 miles east of Cokato

Both the lake and the town were named for an early settler. The town was platted in 1869 when the railroad routed through the area. A station was built about three miles east of Cokato. It would later be torn down and built further west on the south side of the tracks. Having the depot so far out of town was a major contributor to the demise of the town. A turntable was also built. Unfortunately, Smith did not perfect his title to the land, and in 1865 it was pre-empted.

New land owners built a steam mill in 1873, which burned in 1875, was rebuilt and burned again in 1879. Fire was an ever-present danged in early communities.

At its peak, Smith Lake had a population of 150 and included several stores, cooling and watering station, lumber-yard, grain elevator, two-story school, and a saloon. One of the stores was turned into a dance hall, which also burned. As time went on, business declined, buildings were moved or torn down including the depot, which was moved in 1935. Soon all remnants of the town disappeared.

WAVERLY HILLS

1863 - 1870

CLASS A

APPROXIMATE LOCATION:
Absorbed by Waverly

Taking the best land for themselves, the owners of Waverly Mills left the less desirable lands for others, so much so that few settlers could find good claims. Platted in 1856, advertising attracted great attention, partially due to the promise of an excellent water source on the site of a dam built in 1855.

At the time of the Financial Crisis of 1857, the town had the dam and the sawmill nearly done, and the grist mill was under construction. With the crash, all of the partners were out of money and all work was stopped immediately. The owners began quarrelling among themselves and the town lay in ruins. The post office was moved to nearby Waverly Station, and that town became known as Waverly.

PRESERVING HISTORY WRIGHT COUNTY

Nick Neaton, the 4-H director, himself a resident living near the used-to-be community of Oster, developed a "ghost town" project for Wright County's 4-H members. Nick tells of his inspiration for the project:

Growing up in a small town as part of a family that had been in the area for generations, Nick was aware of places that weren't really "there" anymore. Sometimes the places would be churches, bars, creameries, or just a collection of old buildings at a crossroads. In his work with the area 4-H members, he realized that the kids, and their parents, knew little, if anything, about these used-to-be places. Thinking it important to preserve the history of these places and that the youth of the area know more about the history right in their own backyards, he developed his "ghost town" project. Putting together a list of area ghost towns, on which information was available, he spearheaded the process. Students each chose a town, and then conducted research including library research, interviews, visiting the town, and creating a display of the history they had learned. Students presented their findings at the Wright County Fair in 2014, with one student advancing to the Minnesota State Fair.

What a great project, and how wonderful it would be if every county introduced the history to their local youth. One of my favorite sayings is: "It takes the present to preserve the past for the future." Author unknown. Nick and his 4-H members are doing just that.

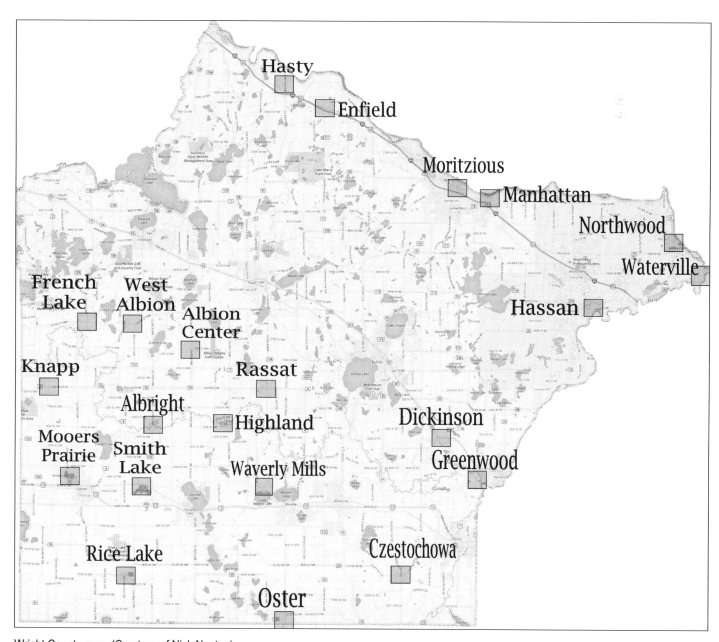

Wright County map. (Courtesy of Nick Neaton)

Yellow Medicine County

Lorne Sign. (Courtesy of Scott Tedrick)

Former Lorne School. (Courtesy of Scott Tedrick)

BURR

1894 – 1907 and 1908 - 1953

CLASS A

APPROXIMATE LOCATION:
From Canby:
MN 68 West for 4.3 miles
Right on 150th Street for 2 miles
Farms and a rural residences in the area

Starting slowly, it took several years for Burr to develop into a bustling community. Originally called Stanley, from its inception until a post office was established in 1894, the town name had to be changed because Minnesota already had a Stanley post office. The new name chosen was Burr.

The only activity those very first years was grain buying. As the Yellow Medicine history book states, area farmers were anxious to have a trading center in the area, so Alfred Froberg opened a store in 1895. Froberg would serve as postmaster from 1895 until 1907, when the post office was discontinued. A year later, in 1908, the post office would be reinstated with a new storekeeper and a new postmaster.

Soon other businesses joined the community, among them a lumberyard in 1901, a second lumberyard in 1903, and the railroad depot (with telegraph services) in 1907. Grain was still the main commodity, and the elevator was the largest business in Burr. At one time, the town housed three elevators.

In 1901, two developers came to Burr and platted another six acres, quickly auctioning them off. The Canbry newspaper reported that every house in Burr was occupied. Incentives were available for anyone who would build a house or business. A construction boom ensued, and three homes were built. Still the total number of homes in Burr was less than a dozen.

Burr did have a bank from 1918 to 1925. Records report that in 1922, there was an robbery attempt. Would-be thieves cut the telegraph line before wrecking the small safe. They abandoned their plans when an area resident started his car to go for help. Due to the bank's small volume of holdings, the bank shut down in 1925.

The post office was discontinued in 1953 at which time it was reported that the eleven boxholders became part of the Canby mail route. Three years later, in 1956, the store closed, and Burr became a rural farm and residential hamlet.

LORNE

1905 – 1935

CLASS C

APPROXIMATE LOCATION:
2 miles south of Granite Falls on Highway 23

Sometimes what goes around comes around. Back in the late 1890s, B.J. and Suzie Aakre donated land to District 92 for a schoolhouse to be built upon. The original school house burned in 1911, and in 1912 a new building was constructed to replace that first school. One hundred fifteen years later, the former school, on that parcel of land donated by the Aakres, once again became the property of an Aakre, B.J. and Suzie's granddaughter Maureen Aakre-Ross. Aakre-Ross bought the former school and the parcel of land it sat on in 2013. The building, which had also served as the Minnesota Falls Town Hall was no longer needed by the township as advances in electronic voting technology no longer required the building be used as a polling place.

In its earliest days, the school had been the heart of the community, which began in the late 1880s. In 1888, the Great Northern Railroad laid tracks from Hanley Falls to Granite Falls and right through Minnesota Falls. Local famers, in 1895, petitioned for a station to be established in the township. Three years later, the Great Northern Railroad purchased seven acres and established a station.

First called Tweed, it was originally a flag stop. Primarily a mail drop, a flag stop allowed a train to snatch bags of mail from an arm alongside the tracks. Incoming mail would be tossed from the train as it passed by. Boarding a train was another matter and could be downright dangerous, If a passenger wanted to board the train, he would stand in the middle of the tracks, waving his arms. The train engineer would sound a signal in response. The passenger would then get off the tracks and wait by the station for pick up. There was also a series of whistles to signal a debarking passenger.

Once a post office was established in 1900, the town's name was changed to Fraserville. For several years the only activity was grain buying. A new elevator had been built by the London Milling Company, associated with the Pillsbury companies.

In 1901, the town consisted of one house and one store. There was space for a dance hall on the second story of the store. Soon other businesses joined the community including another store, lumberyard, two more elevators, blacksmith, and stockyard. In 1905 the town changed names again, this time to Lorne. With time and advances in transportation, the town slowly declined. In 1935 the post office was discontinued. The last elevator was razed in 1958. The old thirty-two-by-twenty-four-foot school became the Minnesota Falls Town Hall. The historic building with rich hardwoods, old kitchen and even the original blackboards was well cared for and maintained by the township.

When no longer needed, the township sold the building and Aakre-Ross completed the ownership cycle. She plans to renovate the building and is making necessary updates. She lives adjacent to the building, in an 1880s-era house that was once Hay's Store. Aakre-Ross hopes to create a community space and to give "the village of Lorne a place to unite community again." Several events and special occasions are slated to be held at the historic building. Once again the 115-year-old building will be at the heart of the community, at the heart of Lorne.

MINNESOTA FALLS

1872 - 1883

CLASS A

APPROXIMATE LOCATION:
Within the bend of the Minnesota River
2 miles below Granite Falls

Once Yellow Medicine County officially became a county in 1871, the competition began. Several towns vied for designation as the new entity's county seat. The area's three largest communities, Yellow Medicine City, Granite Falls, and Minnesota Falls all entered the chase, and the race was on.

Minnesota Falls, once the area's most populated and one of the most important, hastily built a boarding house to accommodate a construction crew. The town's promoters offered a parcel of land for the courthouse as well as the needed paper goods, forms and supplies. In addition, rumor had it that the Hastings and Dakota Railway would cross the river at Minnesota Falls, ensuring added prominence and importance.

In June of 1872, Yellow Medicine City was designated the county seat. Still Minnesota Falls prospered and by 1873 the town had a sawmill, flour mill, several stores, a lawyer's office, blacksmith, doctor, drug store and hotel. A newspaper also operated for a few years. Located at the head of navigation for the Minnesota River, the community was visited by the region's first steamer, the Osceola. For a few years, the steamer brought goods in and departed loaded with four on its return trip.

In 1874, it was decided to move the county seat from Yellow Medicine City to Granite Falls. Minnesota Falls lobbied for the seat and with a 180 residents compared to Granite Falls 50, was certainly the populated site. However, a large rural population that favored Granite Falls, swayed the election. With the newly-designated county seat just a few miles away, Minnesota Falls struggled to survive. It was a long battle, but eventually stores and residents moved to Granite Falls on a steady basis.

A series of misfortunes plagued the declining Minnesota Falls with the 1880's being especially hard years. Fire destroyed the mill, a flood in the spring of 1881 took out the bridge and washed out the town. In June of that same year, the hotel burned to the ground. The church was made into a warehouse. The grocery store was the last business to leave town. Minnesota Falls was no more.

In 1906, a dam was constructed. The land was later sold to Montevideo Power and Light, later known as Northern States Power and was used until 1960.

NORMANIA

1906

CLASS A

APPROXIMATE LOCATION:
From Cottonwood:
County Road 10 for ½ mile, Left on 290th for ¼ mile
Continue for 5 miles, Right on US 59N for 2 miles

With an ideal location along the banks of the Yellow Medicine River, hopes were high for the small rural settlement. The community's first business was the Normania Implement Company. There are no postal records. Little else is known about the short-lived community.

SILLIARDS

1872 - 1887

CLASS G

APPROXIMATE LOCATION:
Just west of Hanley Falls
Now part of Hanley Falls

Sparse records tell little about Sillard other than the fact that it was an early historic community noted as a stopping place for travelers.

The Silliard post office was established in 1872. Twelve years later, when Hanley Falls was established the Silliard post office moved to the new community, keeping the Silliard name until 1887 when the name was changed to Hanley Falls. Eventually Sillards was absorbed by Hanley Falls.

Sorlien Mills

1879 - 1896

CLASS A

APPROXIMATE LOCATION:
5 miles above the mouth of the Yellow Medicine River on 590th Street Minnesota Falls Township

In the summer of 1871, early settler Jacob Jacobson lived in a sod house just southwest of Hanley Falls. Twice a month he would walk to Yellow Medicine City to get supplies, always following the river. He took notice that the river looped coming back within 400 feet of itself. Jacob told folks about the geography and of the possibility of harnessing that water power. Checking it out, the Sorlien brothers looked the land over and thought it perfect for a flour mill. They quickly bought thirty acres of the land and set about building a mill. They sold their farm, bought one adjoining their newly purchased acreage and moved the entire family to the site.

A post office was established and the mail rout between Granite Falls and Redwood Falls serviced Sorlien Mills once a week.

Until 1850, the entire Sorlien family lived as one large family, under one pocketbook. As the brothers got older, married and started raising their own families they decided to divide everything and each went his own ways. Two went to Redwood Falls (with their parents) and set up a mill. Another became an area banker.

The Prestegaard Bridge, near the old grist mill site of Sorlien Mills was controversial in the region for a long time. The steel and concrete, wood-planked bridge was built in 1909. By 1952 the bridge, was closed so necessary repairs could be made. It was reopened in 1955. Scott Tedrick, of *The Granite Falls News* reported that the bridge was closed for good in 2007 and was torn down in 2013, ending years of enmity within the community.

Stavenger

1870 - 1903

CLASS A

APPROXIMATE LOCATION:
Normania township

Though lasting thirty-three years, little is known about Stavenger named for a province in Norway. Rural Free Delivery would signal the end of this rural community.

Stony Run

1873 - 1883

CLASS A

APPROXIMATE LOCATION:
Stony Run Township Section 8

Lasting just a few years, Stony Run was organized in 1871 and an post office was established in 1873. Early settler K.E. Neste began with a fourteen-by-sixteen-foot log cabin with a sod roof. Soon he built a larger one in 1872. The new cabin was two-stories, sixteen by twenty-eight feet with a sixteen-by-sixteen-foot wing. Neste opened a general store. Trading for wheat, he would haul the grain to Benson and bring back goods and supplies. Later joined by his brother, they would operate the store until 1875 when they moved it to Granite Falls. Slowly the town faded away.

In the early years, when Granite Falls and Yellow Medicine City were in heated competition for the county seat, stolen courthouse records were hidden in a Stony Run haystack until Granite Falls was designated the new Yellow Medicine County seat, when, surprisingly, the records were found

YELLOW MEDICINE CITY

1866 – 1870s

CLASS A

APPROXIMATE LOCATION:
South side of the Yellow Medicine River
1 mile west of the site of the Upper Sioux Agency (County
Highway 67)

An early historian, Arthur P. Rose, noted that wherever Native Americans gathered in large numbers, the same locations were selected by settlers to establish their centers of population. Such was the case with Yellow Medicine City, the oldest and largest city in Yellow Medicine County. Just across the river from the newly established city was the location where, from 1854 to 1862, the Dakota had congregated in great numbers. This area was even known as the Dakota capitol.

Yellow Medicine City, founded in 1866, was platted in 1869. Located on the south side of the Yellow Medicine River, the plat had fifteen blocks, twelve numbered and three lettered (A, B, C). Each lot was fifty by 140 feet bounded by streets eighty feet wide and alleys twenty feet wide.

Even though Yellow Medicine County was the only trading center in the area, growth was slow. Yellow Medicine County itself was sparsely populated at the time. Lots were given to anyone who would build a store, shop or home and several new buildings resulted. Early businesses included two stores, a lawyer's office, saloon, hotel, blacksmith, wagon shop, and later a grist mill.

In 1871, Yellow Medicine County was established and Yellow Medicine City was designated the county seat which would prove to be quite a story, complete with thievery and dastardly deeds, and would hasten the demise of the town. That story, summarized from several Yellow Medicine books, records and resources is as follows:

Once designated a county seat, the expectations were that a courthouse would be built within a reasonable time period. Land had been donated for the courthouse, yet no progress was being made and no construction had begun. Yellow Medicine City had only forty residents, so raising funds for to pay for the building had to have been, at the very least, difficult.

Nearby Granite Falls and Minnesota Falls, both had eyes on the county seat designation and both made plans to wrest the title from Yellow Medicine City. Henry Hill, a member of the Minnesota Legislature and prominent Granite Falls resident, put his plan into action in the winter of 1873.

Agreeing to donate land, Hill began to raise money. He also proposed legislation to move the county seat from Yellow Medicine City to Granite Falls. The bill passed the legislature and a heated electoral contest ensued. Minnesota Falls sought the designation but Granite Falls won. The results were contested by Yellow Medicine City to no avail. Eventually the district court ruled in favor of Granite Falls.

Tired of all the legal finagling, a group from Granite Falls took matters into their own hands. On a cold winter's night they set out on a dastardly deed to steal the courthouse records. The group, with blackened faces, gathered the fastest team of horses in the area. Hitching the team to a lumber wagon, they wrapped the wagon wheels with burlap to prevent the wheels from squeaking on the frozen ground. Parking on a high hill over Yellow Medicine City, the men, leaving one man behind to watch the wagon, broke into the office holding the county records. Taking all they could find, they hastily made their retreat. Wrapping the records in canvas, they took them to nearby Stoney River and hid them in a haystack. An extensive search was mounted. Armed with search warrants, many Granite Falls homes were searched. Yet nothing was found. No trace of the records could be found. When Granite Fall's county seat designation was ordered, the missing records surprisingly turned up. The identity of the masked bandits was never revealed.

County seat designation aside, Yellow Medicine City had never kept pace with Granite Falls or Minnesota Falls and the loss of the county seat hastened the demise of the town.

PADDLING THEATER

It's history like you've never seen it before! Combining the story, the tales, the ecology, setting and local lore, Placebase Productions creates unique, interactive, live-action theater that is one hundred percent community based.

Taking a page from the Yellow Medicine County history books, Placebase Productions brought the contentious 1870s county seat battle to life in May of 2013. The live action enactment was a joint venture with Clean Up The River (CURE), the Minnesota Department of Natural Resources and Wilderness Inquiry.

Co-directors Ashley Hanson and Andrew Gaylord started the multi-step process with a series of community meetings, development planning and historical research. Once the basics are determined and the research done, a script, including original music, is created. For the Paddling Theater production, Andrew Gaylord wrote the script and music. Once the writing process is

Arriving canoes. (Photographer Robert Gaylord. Courtesy of Andrew Gaylord and Placebase Productions)

Canoe audience. (Photographer Robert Gaylord. Courtesy of Andrew Gaylord and Placebase Productions)

done auditions and rehearsals begin in earnest. Thirty-four cast members, six site locations along an eight-mile stretch of the river including an island, river bluff, meadow and campground are chosen. Many of the actors and stage crew are local residents.

Audience members arrive at each locale by canoe. Using eighteen voyageur canoes, each holding ten people, the audience travels to each scene location. Cast members perform the scene, then as the canoes go to the next locale, cast members are off and running to the next site.

Seeing history brought to life, the audience and participants are transported back in time. All agree that the adventure is a unique and unforgettable journey to the past. Post production evaluations, a key component to the process, are complimentary and enthusiastic.

Placebase Productions has created other participatory; unique history-based adventures including a September 2014 Bicycling Theater that featured the history of the Fergus Falls State Hospital.

Shore location. (Photographer Robert Gaylord. Courtesy of Andrew Gaylord and Placebase Productions)

Paddling to the next locale. (Photographer Robert Gaylord. Courtesy of Andrew Gaylord and Placebase Productions)

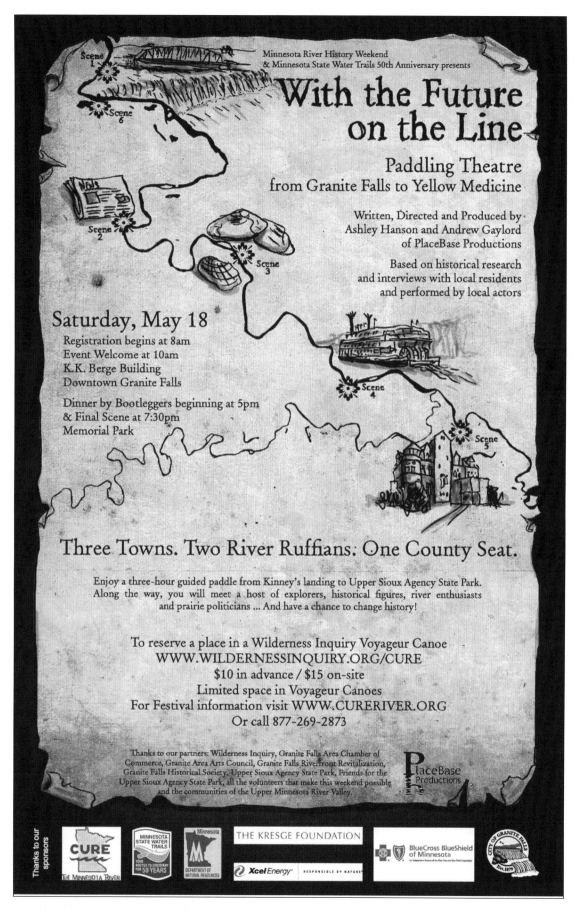

A poster advertising the paddling theater. (Photographer Robert Gaylord. Courtesy of Andrew Gaylord and Placebase Productions)

RECOMMENDED READING

If you are interested in reading a fictionalized account of the history covered in this book, I highly recommended Candace Simar's Abercrombie Trail series. Candace has written a four-part series that is historically accurate, well-researched and a joy to read, for anyone who wants to know more about the times and places, for anyone that loves a good story. The following titles are in the series:

Abercrombie Trail

A fictionalized account of the Sioux Uprising of 1862, inhabited by the nineteenth-century settlers of west central Minnesota. It centers on the life of Evan Jacobson, an immigrant Norwegian stage coach driver.

Pomme de Terre

Newlyweds Serena and Gust settle at Pomme de Terre and look forward to having a family. But government payments to the Indians are late, and the bloody war begins. Serena hates being away from her birth family, but she and Gust find nearby friends.

Birdie

Birdie continues the story of Ragna Larson, kidnapped with her little sister during the 1862 Sioux Uprising. At the end of the conflict, Ragna is returned to Camp Release. Her sister is never heard from again.

Blooming Prairie

Widow Serena Gustafson returns to Pomme de Terre where her husband was killed during the Sioux Uprising. Her dreams of financial independence dissolve when land values plummet after a scourge of Rocky Mountain locusts. Serena must release the past before she can embrace her future.

All are available at North Star Press Press www.northstar-press.com and www.candacesimar.com

BIBLIOGRAPHY

Aakre-Ross, Maureen. "Lorne." Phone. August 22, 2014

Abrahamson, Dean E. *Images of America, Enfield, A Swedish-American Farm Community 1850–2002*. Mount Pleasant. 2003.

Abrahamson, Dean E. Email. July 16, 2014

Anderson, Jim. "Cottage Grove's historic 1840s limestone kiln collapses after flooding." *Minneapolis StarTribune*. July 1, 2014. Web. September 1, 2014.

Anoka County Historical Society. *Anoka County, Minnesota*. Dallas. 1982.

"Arcola Mills – the Origins." http://arcolamills.org

Assumption Catholic Church. *A history of Assumption Church in Eden Valley*. Eden Valley. 1971.

Atwood, E.H. "Early history of Maine Prairie, Fair Haven, Lynden, Eden Lake and Paynesville." St. Cloud.

Balau, Cheryl. "Forest City Memories." N.d.

Balk, Linda. Renville County History. Email. September 4, 2013.

Barbery, Lillian. "The History of French Lake." Unpublished manuscript. June 20, 1974.

Barka, Bridget. "Once upon a town: The story of Strout, MN, 1862–1988." Unpublished. Litchfield. 1988.

Barrett, J.O. "Maudada." N.d. files of Traverse County Historical Society.

Benton County. "The History of Benton County." www.co.benton.mn.us. December 20, 2013.

Bergstron, Vernon & McGriff, Marilyn. *Isanti County Minnesota: An Illustrated History*. Braham. 1985.

"Bertha Carpenter rode "Dinky train" from Stiles Station. Unknown. January 4, 1978.

Bihrle, Craig. "There's a little bit of Irish in Padua." *Sauk Centre Herald*. March 25, 1982.

Big Stone County Historical Society. Brochure. 2013.

"Boomtowns to Ghost Towns." Presentation. Scott County Historical Society. 2006.

Biorn, Wendy. Carver County History. Email. September 9, 2014.

Bradford, Corwin. "Old Anoka County, Soderville past lives on, preserves sense of Community." *Anoka County Union*. August 18, 1989.

"Brief History of Eden Lake Township & Eden Valley, Luxemburg Township & St. Nicholas Manannah Township & Manannah Forest Prairie Township & Watkins." Social 8. 1974.

Brinkman, Marilyn. Interview of Bertha Carpenter. February 2, 1987.

Boulay, Pete. "The Lost City of Gladstone." Maplewood. 1997.

Brainard, Dudley S. "Nininger, a boom town of the fifties." *Minnesota History* Vol 13, Number 2, June 1932

"Brennyville Store Cheese Factory Destroyed by Fire." *Benton County News*. 1947.

"Brief History of Eden Valley." *Eden Valley Boomer*. 1911

Brown, Curt. "Lutefisk: A holiday stinker (but a keeper). *Minneapolis StarTribune*. December 20, 2008.

Busch, Edna Mae. "The History of Stevens County." Unknown.

"Cable, an old landmark." *St. Cloud Daily Times*. Unknown. N.d.

Carley, Kenneth. *The Sioux Uprising of 1862*. St. Paul. 1976.

"Carver County Scrapbook: Ghost Towns." www.carvercountyhistoricalsociety.org January 8, 2014.

Casey, Patrick. *The First 100 years: A History of Meeker County*. Litchfield. 1968.

Chermack, Alton. "Georgeville." Email. July 11, 2014.

Cherveny, Tom. "Paddle Theater takes audience on newly-chartered waters in Granite Falls, Minnesota. *West Central Tribune*. May 20, 2013.

Chippewa County Historical Society. "Welcome to Historic Chippewa City." Brochure. May, 25. 2012.

Churchill, Jeanne (Gilbertson). Letter. Pope County Historical Society. June 2004

City of Maple Plain. "Perkinsville." http://mapleplain.com Web. July 3, 2014.

City of Rockford. www.cityofrockford.org Web. June 5, 2014.

Clayton, Cathy. *Arcola: A Pioneer Logging Community on the St. Croix*. 2004.

"Clear Lake Business Damaged." *St. Cloud Times*. December 28, 1988."

"CMT training at Padua; EMT offered locally." *Sauk Centre Herald*. November 20, 1989.

"Copas Settlement in Scandia dates from 1849." *Historical Whisperings*. Washington County Historical Society newsletter. April 2013.

Cray, Starrla. "Ghost towns." *Dassel Cokato Herald-Journal*. April 29, 2013. Web. January 8, 2014.

Curtiss-Wedge, Franklyn. *History of McLeod County*. Chicago. 1917.

"Czestohowa Church marks 100 years of heritage." *Delano Eagle*. June 20, 1984.

"Dakomin Fire." *Wheaton Gazette*. August 15, 1913.

Decker, John. "Lost Towns." Email. February 11, 2013.

Didreckson, Tina. Email. September 2, 2013.

Dies, James. "Henderson Then and Now in the Minnesota River Valley." Hutchinson. N.d.

Downer, Paul. "Discovering the ghost towns of Carver County." *Carver County News*. August 21, 2008.

Dumonceaux, Mildred. "Grove Lake Academy." Pope County Historical Society. N.d.

"Early Dakota County Towns Flourish and then vanish." *Dakota County Tribune*. June 19, 1975.

Engebretson, Pam. "The Story of New Prairie." Pope County Historical Society. 1993.

Engquist, Anna. "Scandia Beginnings." Stillwater. 1974.

Erickson, Beverly. Looking for Information on Fernsleigh Beach. 2011.

Erickson, Beverly. Traverse County. Letter. August 31, 2014.

Estrada, Heron Marquez. "Gone but not forgotten: Ghost towns continue to have a real presence in Carver County." *Minneapolis StarTribune* October 29, 2008.

Farnam D.R. *History of Wright County*. Delano. 1976.

"Father Brenny Buried in town he Founded." *Benton County News*. August 28, 1955.

"Forest City Stockade." www.forestcitystockade.org

Frear, Dan W. "Ghost Towns of Hennepin County." *Hennepin County History*. Winter 1963,

French, C.A. *Condensed History of Wright County 1851–1935*. Delano. 1935.

Gallagher, Karen. *History of Cedar*. 1976.

Gallagher, Marlys. Email. August 21, 2013.

Gallagher, Marlys. Email. September 6, 2013.

Galvin, Mo. Letter. Sherburne County History. September 4, 2013.

Gaylord, Andrew. Paddling Theater, Email. August 27, 2014.

Gaylord, Andrew. Paddling Theater. Email. August 29, 2014.

Genealogy Trails. www.genealogytrails.com.

Gerdes, Ashli. "Frozen in time: Day Fish Company, a lutefisk tradition." www.wjon.com November 27, 2013.

"Ghost Towns: Stearns County Towns that disappeared from the map. Our top five." WJON. www.wjon.com.

"Ghost Towns." Sherburne County Historical Society. N.d.

"Ghost Towns of Stearns County." *Stearns County Historical Society Newsletter*. Vol 5. No. 3, July 1979.

Gilsenan, Thomas. "Lost Towns of Hennepin County." *Hennepin History* Vol. 49 No. 3, Summer 1990.

Goodman, Nancy and Robert. "Joseph R. Brown–Adventurer on the Minnesota Frontier 1820-1849. Rochester. 1996.

Goodrich, Albert M. "The History of Anoka County and the towns of Champlin and Dayton, Minnesota." Minneapolis. 1905.

Gould, Heidi. "Ghost towns of Carver County." www.mnopedia.org December 17, 2013. Web. January 8, 2014.

Gould, Heidi. "Carver County Lost Towns." Email. September 10, 2014.

Granger, Larry. "Joseph R. Brown Minnesota River Center Experience Minnesota River Valley heritage with a focus on the story of Joseph R. Brown." *Minnesota Heritage*. January 2011.

Greater Lake Sylvia Association. "Remembering Lake Sylvia."

"Grove Lake of Yesteryear." Unknown. N.d.

Guelcher, Leslie A. "The History of Nininger, More than just a dream." Stillwater. N.d.

Haggenmiller, Sharon. Email. November 19, 2013.

"Hamlet of Garen once thrived in Forest Lake Township." *Historical Whisperings*. Washington County Historical Society Newsletter. October 2013.

Hansmann, Dorothy. Interview with Mrs. Anton Essler. December 1937. *Sauk Centre Herald*. July 1, 1982.

Hanson, Ashley. Paddling Theater. Email. August 26, 2014.

Hassan Historical Society. "History of Fletcher." www.hassanhistorical.org Web. July 12, 2014.

Hasty, Warren. *Town of Hasty: Wright County, Minnesota*. 2004.

Hauki, Porter and Freeman. "A History of Chisago County 1851–2001. Unknown. 2001.

Helgeson, Larry. "Artichoke Lake." Email. Septmber 9, 2014.

Hermann, Bob. "Forest City Stockade." Interview. September 29, 2014.

Historical Facts of Sibley County. (Reprint). Unknown. 1949.

"History of Crow River Lutheran Church 1861–1961." Belgrade. N.d.

"History of Crow River/Union Grove Township." www.mdmninfo.com

"History of Maine Prairie & Kimball." *Tri-County News*. 1949.

"History of Royalton." www.hillbillyblue.com Web. February 22, 2013.

"Hoffman Country Mart in St. Anna carries many convenience store items." *Stearns-Morrison Enterprise*. April 25, 1989.

Holden, Thomas. "Oshawa." Phone interview. July 24, 2014.

Johnson, Sandy. "Strout." Interview. September 29, 2014.

Juelich, Clarence. Letter. October 2, 2013.

Kandiyhohi County Historical Society. *Centennial History of Kandiyohi County, Minnesota 1870-1970*.

Kandiyohi County Historical Society. *Historic Sites of Kandiyohi County*. Willmar. 2001.

"Ken's Custom Iron brings tradition into modern era." *Stearns-Morrison Enterprise*. April 25, 1989.

Lamson, Frank B. "Cokato, Wright County 1888-1892." Personal Recollections."

Lamson, Frank B. *History of Meeker County*. Peru. 1937.

"Langdon, a railroad village." *Historical Whisperings*. Washington County Historical Society Newsletter. October 2013.

"Langola Minnesota." www.mntreasures.com Web. February 21, 2013.

Lantto, Dave. "Forest City Stockade" Email. September 16, 2013.

Larson, Rahn. "Georgeville concedes to progress." *The Paynesville Press*. December 18, 1985.

Larson, Willard. *Crossroads Communities. The Ghost Towns of Isanti County*. Isanti. 2003.

Le Sueur Bicentennial Book Committee. *Le Sueur, Town on the River*. Marceline. 1977.

Lindblad, Sister Owen. "Skeletons of time." *St. Cloud Times*. October 24, 2000.

Lindquist, Oscar E. *Those Were the Days*. Dassel. Unkown.

Lovoll, Odd S. *Norwegians on the Prairie*. St. Paul. 2007.

Lund, Duane. R. *Our Historic Upper Mississippi*. Staples. 1991.

Lundberg, Ann. Email. September 4, 2013.

Lundberg, Ann. Email. September 6, 2013.

Lundberg, Ann. Email. July 15, 2012.

Lynn, June. Chippewa City. Email. June 19, 2014.

Lynn, June. Chippewa County History. Email. July 10, 2012.

Martens, Ken. *The Perilous St. Croix River Valley Frontier*. Charleston. 2014.

"Maudada." *Wheaton Gazette-Reporter*. November 15, 1918.

"Maudada put up tough fight for Existence." *Wheaton Gazette*. July 27, 1951.

McLeod County Historical Society. *McLeod County History Book*. Dallas. 1979.

McLeod County Historical Society. *The Lost Towns of McLeod County*. Hutchinson. 2010.

McCrossan, Karen. "Fletcher." Email. August 6, 2014.

McCrossan, Karen. Fletcher and Hassan." Phone interview. August 6, 2014.

Marohn, Kristi. "Run-down homes not Georgeville Image." *St. Cloud Times*. May 16, 2000.

Marshall, Linday. "Tracking down the ghost community of Hazelton." *Waconia Patriot*. September 1, 2011.

"The Mayhew Lake People." Unknown. Benton County Historical Society files.

McCrea, Willard F. "Remnants." Unknown. Benton County Historical Society files.

Meeker County Memories. Meeker County Historical Society. Litchfield. 1987.

"Meeker County." www.garminnesota.org.

Meeker County Historical Society. *Meeker County Historic Sites and Places of Interest*. Brochure. N.d.

Meyer, Roy W. "The Story of Forest Mills, A Midwest Milling Company." *Minnesota History*. March 1956.

Miller, Kristen. "Forest City Stockade: A stroll through 1862. *Dassel-Cokato Herald-Journal*. August 13, 2012.

Minnesota Courts. "Lac Qui Parle Courthouse." www.mncourts.gov.

Minnesota Department of Transportation. "Historic Roadside Development Structures Inventory WR-AKT006, Dickenson Spring Roadside Parking Area. N.d. Web. July 12, 2012.

Mitchell, W.B. *History of Stearns County*. Vol. 1. St. Cloud. 1915.

Moen, Gerry. "Lake Stella" Interview. September 29, 2014.

Mohan, Corey. "He's no Bernie Madoff: Meet Ignatius Donnelly and the Ghost Town of Nininger." www.coreymohan.com March 9, 2011. Web. June 1, 2014.

"Montana Cowboy Sticks Up Padua." *St. Cloud Times*. February 16, 1924.

Moran, Mike. "Flap went to high court." *St. Cloud Times*. November 14, 2000.

Morse-Kahn, Deborah. The Historic St. Croix Valley: A Guided Tour. St. Paul. 2010.

Morgan, William Tower. *Earth, Wood, Stone. Central Minnesota Lives and Landmarks*. St. Cloud. 2008.

Myers, Mouraine R. *101 Best stories of Wright County, Minnesota*. Buffalo. 1976.

Myers, Mouraine R. & Jameson, Marion. Wright County Towns. N.d. Files at Wright County Historical Society.

Narvestad, Carl & Amy. *A History of Yellow Medicine County 1872-1972*. Granite Falls. 1972.

Neaton, Nick. "Wright County Lost Towns." Email. September 9, 2014.

Neaton, Nick. 4-H Youth Development–Ghost Towns of Wright County Project. 2014.

Neill, Rev. Edward D. *History of Dakota County and the City of Hastings*. Minneapolis. 1881.

Neill, Rev. Edward D. etal "History of the Minnesota Valley." Minneapolis. 1882.

Neill, Rev. Edward D. "History of the Upper Mississippi Valley." Salem. 1881 Reprint 1994.

Nelson, Bruce. "Real People with message: Times writer listens area hippie Colony." *St. Cloud Times*. August 20, 1969.

Nistler, Michael. D. *The Valley of Eden*. Eden Valley. 1986.

Nistler, Mike. "Everyone turns Irish for Padua parade." *St. Cloud Times*. March 18, 1990.

Nistler, Mike. "Leapin' potato bugs! Padua's St. Pat's parade rolls on." *St. Cloud Times*. March 16, 1985.

Norelius, Theodore. *A History: Sunrise, Kost & Almelund*. North Branch. 1975.

"North Crow River Lutheran Church. 1870–1970." Cokato. 1970.

O'Connell, Jim. "Centsohowa." Phone September 8, 2014.

O'Malley, Rob & O'Brien, Jennifer. "Fremont City, Clearwater's neighbor city, flowered, faded in 1850s." 1985.

Oldendorf, Yvette. "Arcola Mills." Phone. September 17, 2014.

Oldendorf, Yvette. "Arcola Mills." Email. October 31, 2014.

Olson, Sam. "Lac Qui Parle history." Email. September 17, 2014.

Olson, Sam. "Lac Qui Parle history." Email. October 5, 2013.

The Ortonville Independent "Country schools disappear, memories will be preserved" November 26, 2002. Web. September 4, 2013.

Ostby, Mary. "Brennyville." Email. September 21, 2014.

"Padua bar events help feed community spirit." *St. Cloud Times*. August 21, 1988.

"Padua celebrates St. Pat's day." *Sauk Centre Herald*. March 25, 1982.

"Padua's Fall Festival." *Sauk Centre Herald*. September 18, 1980.

"Padua School." *Sauk Centre Herald*. September 7, 1977.

"Padua Reunion." Brochure. July 4, 1982.

Parker, Donald Dean. "Lac Qui Parle, It's Missionaries, Traders and Indians." Brookings. 1964.

Paumen, Elaine. "Fremont City." Unpublished manuscript. September 2014.

Patera, Alan H. & Gallagher, John S. "The Post Offices of Minnesota." 1978.

"Pelican Lake Ballroom has 50 year tradition of entertainment." *Stearns-Morrison Enterprise*. April 25, 1989.

Peterson, Brent. Washington County Lost Towns. Letter. June 9, 2014.

Peterson, Merlin. Pope County History. Email. September 2, 2013.

Phillips, Marty. "Life in Popple Creek Centers on Store." *St. Cloud Times*. N.d.

Placebase Productions. www.placebaseproductions.com.

Plaggerman, Lorie. "Truckin' right along at Hasty." *Wright Way Shopper*. October 16, 1980.

Plaggerman, Lorie. "What makes one town survive and the next one not?" *Wright Way Shopper*. November 27, 1980.

Postal History. http://www.postalhistory.com.

Reicher, Matt. "The Short History of Nininger, Minnesota." www.minnpost.com/mnopedia February 25, 2014. Web. June 24, 2014.

Renville County Historical Society. "Beaver Falls, the Beginning of the County." N.d.

Renville County Historical Society. *Old Villages of Renville County*. 2006.

Renville County Historical Society. *Renville County History Book*. Dallas. 1981.

Rippley, LaVern J. "Minnesota River Valley Ghost Towns." *Currents*. Vol. 1.

"Roads lead to St. Anna and Bill's Bar." *Stearns-Morrison Enterprise*. April 25, 1989.

Rose, Arthur P. *Illustrated History of Yellow Medicine County*. Marshall. 1914.

Ryan, Mackenzie. "Brothers home town faded away with times." *St Cloud Times*. May 13, 2006.

"St. Anna." *Stearns-Morrison Enterprise*. April 25, 1989.

"St. Croix County seat: Dacotah–The dream that never was." *Historical Whisperings*. Washington County Historical Society newsletter. April 2014.

"St. Mary's mission church." *Delano Eagle.* May 28, 1925.

"St. Mary's marks 100 years." *Delano Eagle.* June 13, 1984.

"San Francisco." www.ghostowns.com. June 3, 2013

Sauk Rapids Sentinel "Quarter of a Century Ago." June 26, 1930

Schmitz, Jacob. "Traverse County, Telling It the Way Things Were." Unknown.

Schulz, Brian. "Yellow Medicine County." Email. July 15, 2012.

Schwartzer, Walt. "Centsohowa." Phone. September 8, 2014.

Sherburne County Heritage. Sherburne County Historical Society. Dallas. 1986.

Sherman, Hila. *Bayport–Three little towns on the St. Croix 1842-1976.* Hudson. 1976.

Sibley County Historical Society. *The Henderson to Fort Ridgely Trail.* 2003 Edition. Henderson 200.

Sibley County Sesquicentennial Committee. *Bits and Pieces – Celebrating 50 Years of Sibley County History.* Hutchinson. 2003.

Skaja-Bell, Paulie. *Rogers, Hassan Township, and Fletcher Remembered.* Charleston. 2006

Smith, Glanville. "Historicals go pioneering." March 1950.

Sowa, Edward. "The Town of Medora. Benton County." Unknown. Benton County Historical Society files.

Sowa, Edward F. "Williamsville, Minnesota. Benton County." Unknown. Benton County Historical Society files.

Sparrow, Magdalene R. *Big Stone County, Minnesota 1881-1981.* Ortonville 1981.

Stanley, Duane D. *Our Early Years on Maine Prairie: Pioneer Beginnings of the Kimball Community.* Kimball. 2006.

Stearns County Historical Society. "The History of Padua & St. Anthony's Church." *Crossings.* September 1997. Vol. 23, No. 5.

Stelling, Linda. "Georgeville loses historic building." *The Paynesville Press.* October 4, 2014.

Straumanis, Andris. "Patchwork, Ethnicity along the way" *Elk River Star News.* June 26, 1984.

Sturdevant, Andy. "Exploring a Carver County ghost town, San Francisco, Minn." www.minnpost.com November 27, 2013. Web. January 8, 2014.

Sturdevant, Andy. "Nininger City, Ignatius Donnelly's lost Atlantis on the Mississippi." www.mnpost.com March 26, 2014. Web. June 10, 2014.

Swanson, Kermit. "A Hearty German Tradition." *St. Peter Herald.* November 4, 2004.

Swift County Historical Society. "Swift County Minnesota–Collection of Historical Sketches and Family Histories." Dallas. 1979.

Tedrick, Scott. "Iconic Minnesota Falls township hall up for sale. *Granite Falls Advocate Tribune.* July 18, 2013.

Tedrick, Scott. "Love of Lorne brings life to Minnesota Falls town hall." *Granite Falls Advocate Tribune.* July 14, 2014.

Tedrick, Scott. "The Prestegard Bridge Near old Sorlien Mills torn down." *Granite Falls Advocate Tribune.* March 8, 2013.

Tedrick, Scott. "Yellow Medicine County keeping on top of bridge maintenance." *Granite Falls Advocate Tribune.* February 4, 2014.

Thielen, Lois. "St. Anna residents still consider their community a village." *Stearns-Morrison Enterprise.* January 2, 1979.

Thompson, Richard S., Monson, Steven J. *The Taylors Falls & Lake Superior Railroad.* St. Louis Park. 2005.

Thurn, Karl and Helen. *Round Robin of Kandiyohi County.* Raymond. 1958.

Traverse County Historical Society. *Wheaton Centennial Book.* Wheaton. 1987.

"Traverse County Memories." Unknown. N.d.

Trustheim, Jan. "Padua reunion a success." *Sauk Centre Herald.* July 22, 1982.

Upham, Warren. "Minnesota Place Names http://mnplaces.mnhs.org.

"Vicksburg." www.ghosttowns.com July 9, 2012. Web. July 8, 2013.

Washington County Historical Society. *A History of Washington County–Gateway to Minnesota History.* Stillwater.

"Watab Minnesota and the Peace Rock." www.heschhistory.blogspot.com Web., January 15, 2013.

"Watab (Benton County)" www.mntreaures.com Web. July 12, 2013.

Webb, Rebecca. "What secret treasure lies in Pope County's long forgotten Cheesetown safe?" *Senior Perspective.* November 200?.

Weckwerth, Debbie. "New Rome, Once a Thriving Village." Unknown.

"Whatever happened to Unity, Minnesota?" *Crossings,* Stearns County Historical Society. June/July 1992.

"What's in a name?" *Eden Valley-Watkins Voice.* January 8, 2014.

"Wheaton Centennial Book." Unknown. 1987.

"When the Audience Paddles Up to the Play." www.cnn.com

Wolter, Russell. "St. Anna field receives face lift." *St. Cloud Citizen Times.* December 8, 2002.

Woodcock, Elijah. F. "Stories of E.T. and Loretta Woodcock." 1961.

Wulff, Mrs. Walter. "Big Stone County History." Chokio. 1959

"Yesteryears." *The Monticello Times.* May 8, 1975.

"Yesteryears." *The Monticello Times.* July 24, 1975

"Yesteryears." *Cokato Enterpise.* February 26, 1976.

"Youths to revive Georgeville Trading Post." *The Paynesville Press.* February 13, 1969.

Zeuge, Unsie. "Carver County's "ghost cities" gone. *Chanhassen Villager.* October 27, 2005.

INDEX